Prison Psalms

Ellen Adele Harper

Introduction

The ego is an artifice, an interface between us and the world. The ego is the lens through which we look out upon the world of our experience, but it is a distorted lens, rather like a funhouse mirror, tinted by our beliefs, our feelings, and our mindset. My false ego was male, built of a lifetime of repression.

This manuscript marks the beginning of a seven-year period of introspection. For seven years I would peel away the layers of this false onion. Whenever my ego tried to distract me from this task—which was often—circumstances would force me back to the grindstone. It was as if this whole experience of seven-years duration was intentional, and that it was, though the intention was all mine. By the time these years had passed, all of the layers of that onion had been peeled back to reveal the essential truth: the true me. After seven years, I stepped out of prison the woman I truly am.

This entire transformation occurred in prison, where I was sent on ridiculous charges, given a long sentence because I had fought the charges for four years. If I could go back and relive the past decade, I would not change a thing. The entire experience, though it left me with emotional scars, was necessary to uncovering and admitting my truth.

I wrote this manuscript in one month, while the entire prison was grappling with a norovirus epidemic. While everyone around me was grievously ill, I worked on this manuscript, finding the insights that would usher me down the path of self-discovery. By the time I had finished the manuscript, which coincided roughly with the end of the epidemic, I had written over 1,000 poems. The spirit of these poems allowed me to transcend the prison walls, at the same time opening my heart to reveal all the love it contained. It is my hope that these poems, and all my writings, will help to elevate the readers as well, if they are open to it.

I cherish the truth of myself, which was subjugated all of my life by a society that said such truths were taboo, that said my identity must revolve around my genitalia. This was just another layer in the onion of false identity, albeit a layer near to the heart. It was stripped away in the end. While there was certainly emotional pain involved in this process—the ego cries out as it is skinned, and will do everything in its power to halt the process and save itself—there was underneath it all the joy of freeing myself from oppression, and the deep and abiding love that lay at the core of my eternal truth. In the end I emerged, like Aphrodite born of a clamshell, a trans woman in love with life and united in the truth that the same light that shines within her, shines within all beings and all things, uniting all that exists.

Beyond these few words, I allow these poems to speak for themselves. Welcome to my process of transformation. It is my hope that they will help you to find your own eternal truth. I wish to bless you as I have been blessed by the circumstances of my life, which are no less and no more than an expression of that truth, as recognized when you remove the lens of the false ego. For that self-truth is the source of all strength, all talent, all well-being, and all love. May you be blessed to discover it within this lifetime.

***

Fans of my spoken word performances will want to hear me say more about prison and being trans. Never disappoint your audience. I can do no worse than to quote the conclusion of my prison novel, Effing the Ineffable. Accordingly, this is the effing conclusion.

Daniel lay on the bunk that night, looking back on the last seven years. Seven years of prison that led directly to this bunk in this dilapidated hotbox of a unit. Seven years of struggle in the effort not to lose his life—or his soul—all leading to this point, this moment? The future was a blank; in fact, this moment seemed more like an ending than a beginning. He had no home, no family, no career. The only thing he had going for him was his winning personality and a pile of handwritten manuscripts—wonderful writings certainly—but many of them so esoteric that their appeal would be extremely limited. They were the record of seven years of introspection; seven years spent tearing away at all the false layers of identity, like peeling through the layers of an onion, to find the eternal truth within.

And he had found that truth. In the end, it had been easy enough, for he had lived with that truth all of his life; it was the truth that shone out through his being as himself. At his core, stripped of all else, he was existence, consciousness, and bliss. He was a light of love and joy, looking out upon this experience as a faceted and multidimensional expression of himself, tarnished by belief systems both accepted from society and maintained by himself. He cherished that light; it was golden, it was the philosopher's stone. It was the vital essence of all existence, and it sang in the unitary chorus of all things. But that wasn't who he was: he was the expression of that light—that existence, consciousness, and bliss—in this moment of experience. And what was the essence of that expression, what was the essence of his personal identity?

Funny: he had undertaken the monumental work of finding his truth and establishing himself within it so that he would be ready to face the life he would be released into at the end of seven years. Yet now he felt further from that truth than ever. Everything about the past seven years had kept him focused on finding his truth, tearing away all the false layers of identity. Much of it had been painful, with the uncovering of past traumas, and terrible decisions on his own part. He felt like he hadn't really had much choice in the matter; circumstances drove him at this task like a relentless grindstone. Had it all happened to bring him to this moment, where he was hopelessly lost, without mooring, anchor or rudder?

He remembered that tarot reading Mighty El had done for him to help him make the decision of whether to transfer to this institution. The reading said that he could stay at Loretto and be comfortable for the rest of his life in the identity he had made for himself there, but never find the truth—never discover who he really was. Or he could come here, where the last vestige of false ego would be torn away from him to reveal the truth, and in revealing that truth, he would find himself and would receive the world. Well, that last vestige of ego had been brutally ripped away in the events that led him to the SHU, but what had he found. Instead of discovering anything, he felt lost and bereft. Yet, in an odd way, he did feel closer to that truth than ever. Still, it would not be correct to say that he was pure existence, consciousness and bliss. He was that, but that was not the unalterable core of his identity; it was the light that shone through that identity into the world of his experience.

His experience in the SHU had been seminal and inescapable in ways he could not understand. Without a doubt, he was not the same person who entered the SHU. What was it about his month with Isabella that had altered him so fundamentally and permanently? Isabella stood at the hub of that month, yet why did she have such a prominent position in his life? He did love her. They had helped each other through some of the worst moments of their lives. Such an experience could not help but solidify a strong bond between them. But it was more than that. His attraction to Isabella was much more than that. All of his thoughts now seemed drawn to her, like moths to a light. What was it about her? Unless, as he well knew, it wasn't about her.

Daniel knew that all of our experiences are ultimately about us: they are our expression of ourselves upon the circumstance with which we are presented in this moment. Every person we meet in our experience is, in our experience, an expression of ourselves in response to that person. Always, with no exception. So why was Isabella so important, so central to him?

Daniel could not avoid talking about her to his new cellie. He was, after all, rather obsessed with her, and struggling to determine the nature and meaning of this obsession. His new roommate was a Christian fundamentalist. He said Isabella was possessed by Jezebel, and in spending a month with her Daniel had been poisoned. But now that his roommate had revealed the truth to him, he could free himself from her grasp by praying to God for delivery. That was ridiculous; Isabella was no demon. She was confused, yes, and possibly psychotically disturbed. But the reason why she exerted such a hold over him lay not in her, as Daniel well knew, but in him.

Like all truths which our egos try to protect us from, it had only to be admitted. The ego keeps us from this truth not for our sake but for its own, as we must cast the ego aside in order to embrace these essential truths. But what truth lay behind the play of his month in the SHU, waiting to be found once he parted the curtain of his own ego. It was a truth he had lived with his entire life. It was a truth that colored his entire life, without ever being admitted. Yet it was a truth known to him, known throughout his life back to his earliest years, so that it was the tinting of his most basic and essential identity. Now it was time to admit this truth and embrace it.

Isabella had intuited this truth when she first met him. It was a kinship between them. She had told him she thought he was really a woman, and in his heart, when she said this, he knew the truth of it. He was a woman; he was a she.

He had the soul of a woman. That was the truth: his very nature was feminine, and always had been. And with this realization, everything fell into place: his alienation as a child, and his own rejection of anything male—sports, automobiles, machismo. Yes, he had lived a life of male privilege, for which he would be eternally apologetic. But that male privilege went with a male identity which had mistakenly been thrust upon him by a society that believed his identity lay in his sex organs. It was a false image that became subconsciously rolled up into his ego, but it was not who he really was.

This was one reason why Isabella was so important to him: she was an expression of his anima. She was a trans woman who had admitted her truth and now lived it, whatever the circumstances. The strength that was required of her to do so was without comparison; it was the strength to face all ridicule and all attacks of male privilege outraged at her betrayal, even to the point of raping her. It endured because this strength drew from the core of her true identity. For standing in her truth, Isabella should be honored instead of vilified, as his cellie had done. And this truth shown its light upon the truth within him, drawing forth tones of sympathetic harmony.

In this moment, without being wholly aware of what was happening, Daniel was born a woman, nameless and as yet without a voice, but a woman in her essence. Though it would take months until she would be fully admitted, she would never again be exiled to the shadows, for she had been revealed. And in her lay the strength and the talent that was expressed as an artist and shaman. She was he. In truth, there was no he but a fiction forced upon him and then accepted by him, first in false shame, and then in an effort to hide from the shame and alienation that came to him with this role. There was no he but an artifice. There was only she.

This was her future, the one she prepared for in seven years of deep introspection, the future that her false ego tried to run from even as it could not look into. Her future lay in expressing herself honestly as a woman. And in so doing, to express herself with art and intimacy, with all of the craft honed over a lifetime of writing. Now this woman, this poetess would express this truth with a beauty that would touch the heart of readers, to blossom there within the light of their own true selves, whoever they might be. The light of existence within her was the same light of existence to be found in everyone and everything. This light was the drive to individual expression that gave everyone their distinct identity. In her, this most essential individual expression was female, orphaned, abandoned, and suffering a lifetime of misunderstanding and self-ridicule. Only to be born purely of the light of existence, consciousness, and bliss, born from the heart where she had harbored for an entire lifetime, born in and of the light of truth. Now it was time for her to sing this truth so that all would hear.

Ellen Adele Harper
7/13/2022

OPENING SALVOS

1. Where I Stand

are many
there me's

you know at most
only a few

and yet I stand
behind them all

3/7/15

2. Hidden Constellations

constellations
traverse hidden
a sky
of

3/7/15

3. Self-Absorbed Stars

most stars are
so absorbed
in the circumstances
of their illumination
they see not the source
of their own light

3/7/15

4. Self-Igniting

O for the match
to ignite this world
that it might see
by the light
of its own fire

3/7/15

5. Disclosure

by the light
of the fire within me
I can see
the fire within you

3/7/15

6. Free Perspective

chained to this rock　　　　flying freely the skies
locked in this cage　　　　over the distant mountains
where I find myself
in this moment
is only a matter
of my perspective

3/7/15

7. Shaman's Song

on the wings of hawk
I overcome all boundaries
on the breath of white buffalo
I am connected to the heart of the earth
on the wings of dragon
I span the quantum field
on the feet of black jaguar
I move in a sacred manner traversing
the way beyond death
on the feet of fox
I stay hidden keeping what I do here
safe from doubt and interruption
on the wings of mallard
I draw from the waters the resonance
of love
on the tail of peacock
I part the veil between
the physical and the spirit world
on the wings of snowy owl
I spiral upward
into the spirit world
on the wings of the sidhe
I make my place
in the spirit world and there
proclaim my existence

3/7/15

8. Outward Expression

everywhere I look
everything I see
is an outward expression
of divinity

3/7/15

9. From the Heart

from the heart truly
from the heart we live
though we be lost
in the chatter of our brains

3/7/15

BEHIND THE CURTAIN

10. Framing

existence
is a framework
through which awareness
flows

3/8/15

11. Fiction

the wakeaday
world is a fiction
we defend

3/8/15

12. Walls of Sand

our walls are made of sand
each grain of which
is a window looking out upon infinity

3/8/15

13. Insubstantial

each granule of matter
is no more
than a frame of existence
through which
energy flows

3/8/15

14. Gentleman's Agreement

the wakeaday
world is only a matter
of agreement
in every moment
we enter into a contract
with all that exists
seeing only
in each moment what
is agreed upon
yet in the moment
we perceive the contract
in its divine existence
we are freed to enter
into a new agreement
where we are allowed
to write the terms

3/8/15

15. Playwrights

we script
all of our dreams
no less the dream
we call the wakeaday

3/8/15

16. Undefinable

I defy
all definitions

3/8/15

17. Unnamable

the reality
I perceive
can never be
fully named in the very naming
it becomes the thing
not named

3/8/15

FREEDOM

18. In Freedom

in freedom I stand
alone
yet see myself
in everything

3/8/15

19. Freed

in granting freedom
to everything perceived
I am freed

3/8/15

20. Freedom Expressed

freedom is expressed
by the sort of attachment
you make
whether formed
in bondage
or in love

3/8/15

21. Freedom Relinquished

in this moment
I am free
yet this freedom
is lovingly relinquished
in the expression of
my existence

3/8/15

22. Loving Freedom

in love
all are free

3/8/15

KEEP IN MIND

23. Mind Extension

wherever
you might send your mind
in thought
there
some portion of your awareness
does reside

3/9/15

24. In the Pond

be ever mindful
of the waters in the pond
where you swim
and aware
of every current there

3/9/15

25. Friendly Ghosts

we inhabit
a world full of ghosts
but you will only
be haunted
by those
with which you have an affinity

3/9/15

26. The World You Make

the world you perceive
is the story you make
of the stimulus drawn
by your own resonance

3/9/15

27. No Complaint

the complainer lives
in a world he detests
better to bless
the world around you
and by the world
be blessed

3/9/15

28. Prison Halls

make even the halls
of a prison
into avenues
of the divine

3/9/15

29. Hidden Treasure

even mud
and filth
hold a treasure
of the divine

3/9/15

30. Your Light

the world
is illuminated
by the light within
and in this light
you see it

3/9/15

31. State of Being

divinity
is a birthright
and a state of mind

3/9/15

THE SACRED

32. Divine Right

only by granting divinity
to all that exists
do you become divine

3/9/15

33. Recognition

by recognizing the divinity
in everything
you recognize
yourself

3/9/15

34. By Inner Light

the outer world holds
no meaning but in
reflection
it is by the inner
light that you
will be nurtured
let that light shine
in love and you
will prosper

3/9/15

HEROIC QUEST

35. The Hero's Adventure

only ego
and reaction
seeks heroic acts
in slaying outside
villains
true bravery comes
in facing the demons
within that can't
be fought with arms
but only by exposing
the light of love
to reveal them naught
but shadows

3/9/15

36. Cowled Demons

with love unfurl
each shadowed cowl
to reveal the demon
is only your
reflection

3/9/15

37. Loving Steps

where negativity abounds
there must every step
be sacred
and every act
illuminated
with love

3/9/15

38. Anchors Away

it is the petty annoyances
that weigh you down
let them go
and you rise to
the surface
transcend them
and you fly

3/10/15

39. Lost in Matter

knowing what boundless divinity
what loving awareness
resides within all things
how is it
we lose ourselves
in the camouflage

3/10/15

LOVING

40. No One but My Love

no one knows me
but my love and in
her love she knows
me truly

3/10/15

41. The Temper of Love

all that in your world
exists
is seen through the temper
of your love

3/10/15

42. Degrees of Love

all emotions
from fear and anger
to joy and ecstasy
are but degrees of love

3/10/15

TREASURE

43. Treasures of the Heart

when the heart does rule
the mind
O what treasures
you will find

3/10/15

44. Divine Expression

this world is but
an expression
of divine awareness
if you seek divine
awareness then
you seek this world

3/10/15

45. Divine Revelation

I seek not to escape
this world but to reveal
the divinity hidden
within it

3/10/15

46. The World Ran

As a child I caught pollywogs and frogs
I skipped and laughed and played and sang
I raced with the wind
and the world ran with me

as a teen I rebelled against all limitations
I partied and I questioned and I explored
I shouted my name to the wind
and the world shouted with me

as an adult I went to work
I studied and I assayed and most of all I created
I proclaimed my perceptions to the wind
and the world proclaimed with me

and all along I reached for the stars beyond my grasp
I sought fulfillment with visions, art and sex
I found and lost enlightenment
and the world turned with me

Now I approach that door I so long sought
I approach in awareness, with love and joy and compassion
and through the opening door I see the light
and the world is illumined with me

eventually the world that I know will pass
and the people I love, the world I love, the life I love will pass
and yet my awareness will be reborn in this moment eternal
and the world will be reborn with me

3/10/15

47. Hold On, Let Go

holding on is done in fear
and limited perspective
to truly love is to let go
granting the beloved the freedom to shine
in such love the hidden nature
of the beloved is proclaimed
to shine light on the one
until both are revealed naked
reveling in the knowledge
that lover and beloved are one

3/10/15

48. Dance the World

in love I release
the world
reaching
for the light within
in this light
the world and I do dance

3/10/15

MY FATHER

49. Dear Father

dear father
I bid you goodbye
in the waking world
and in the world
of dreams I took
your hand and led
you to the tree
of life
fare you well
in the land beyond
illusions I
will see you soon

3/10/15

50. For My Father

what loving man
gave of his life to provide
for his family
and in the emptiness
of this world finally
took his leave
now he has found
all of the treasures
denied in this life
yet the greatest treasure
that he always held
is love

3/10/15

51. A Loving Light

from my heart
dear father
a loving light
I send you
to speed you on
your way

3/10/15

LOVE LIGHT

52. Love Transcendent

love transcends
space and time
it is the light
that nourishes us
known and all
that I hold dear
it is the light
of all I've ever
known and all
that I hold dear
it is the blessing
I give to all
existence
it is the light
that dances between
the world and myself

3/10/15

53. A Game of Catch

it is a game
of catch
between myself and
the world of my perception
the ball
we pass awareness
between us of love and
is a brilliant light

3/10/15

54. Give Your Blessing

the blessings
freely given
are the blessings
you receive

3/10/15

55. Matters of the Heart

love all matter
transcends spilling
out its essence
to dance
in all awareness

3/10/15

56. This Moment Mine

this moment
is mine
and my awareness
in it
only in this moment the truth revealed
is freedom found love and joy
and in unfettered
allow none
to take this from you
but share it freely
with your blessing

3/10/15

57. To Truly Live

let go of worry
and regret
live in this moment
and allow it to shine
only then will the universe
open itself to you
only then
will you truly live

3/10/15

58. A Light in Darkness

surrounded by ignorance
it is then most
vital to shine
your light

3/10/15

59. Illumination

with darkness others
seek to subdue you
send them blessings
and continue to shine
and in your resonance
eventually you will find
the day illumined

3/10/15

60. Lantern

in darkness keep
your lantern lit

3/10/15

61. For Glory

for glory live
and by its light
illuminate all circumstances

3/10/15

62. The Spacious Present

each second
of time
is an eternal
moment point
in the spacious present
each probability
is itself
a vital
moment point

each moment point
radiates
an infinity
of probabilities
all moment points
exist simultaneously
infinite eternal
radiant in awareness

3/11/15

THE NET

63. Sea of Potentiality

the spacious present
is an unbounded
sea of potentiality
through which
All That Is
is given expression

3/11/15

64. Cosmic Network

each movement
every act
is a spectrum
of moment points
radiating
a cosmic neural network
in a matrix
mirrored physically
of probabilities
in the brain

3/11/15

65. Indra's Net

each second
of our lives
we shift through
probabilities
each shift each moment point
a quantum leap an entirely new creation
into an entirely new born in that singular moment
moment point of awareness
through which we tread
a path of consistency
building the continuity
of our lives

3/11/15

66. Consistency

the only thing that prevents
you from jumping
from here   to here
is your belief
in consistency

3/11/15

67. Textiles

your beliefs   your thoughts
are the dye   and emotions
and the weft   provide
of the warp   the stitching
but the material
is the infinite
quantum field
of the spacious present

3/11/15

68. The Weavers Trade

an experienced weaver learns
to weigh every stitch
and how to work in
bangles to compliment the weave

3/11/15

69. Were not for Love

were it not for love
there would be no
existence
were it not for love
there would be no
reason to exist

3/11/15

70. Sun Lover

be not miserly
with your love
to guard it is
to choke it
give of it freely
that it be a sun
to nurture all existence

3/11/15

71. Nurturing Net

you are connected
to everything that
exists better to
make it a net
of love

3/11/15

72. My Father's Journey

I led my father to the crossroads
and there bid him adieu
I helped him to pack his bags
and directed him to the intersection

I guided my dad to board his ship
unfurling his sails
and as he set out on those gentle waters
I was the last one to whom he called

he spoke to me from the threshold
to assure me he now understood
there are no endings here
rather an awakening from the dream called life

I brought my dad to the world tree
where the detritus of this life
the compost of this life
is broken down to feed the roots

we climbed among the branches
and picked the golden fruits
and when we gained the crown of the tree
my dad rose up to touch the stars

and there in the fullness
of love and vitality
I left him though in love and in truth
he has never left me

3/12/15

73. A Truer World

the world of our dreams is truer
and more vital
though we confine it to our sleep
there hidden
in the fecund darkness
of the night
from the stark poverty
of day

there we touch upon
the greater reality
the limitless boundless
infinity of existence
that cannot be contained
within the linearity
of our physical wakeaday
existence

3/12/15

UNSEEN EYES

74. Shade Your Eyes

we shade our eyes
from the greater glory
that we might focus
upon the minutia of this life

3/12/15

75. Not by Our Brains

not our brains but our hearts
conduct our awareness
not by our intellect but by our imagination
are we introduced to the secrets of existence
not by our egos but by our love
are we connected to All That Is

3/12/15

76. The Fullness of Time

the fullness of time is not measured
by the beating
of a clock but in
the beating of our heart

3/12/15

77. Our Eyes Blind Us

our eyes blind us
if you would perceive
truly then look
with your heart

3/12/15

78. Feel not See

if you would truly
know the world
then feel it
do not see it

3/12/215

79. Prejudice

the outer sight perceives
objectively
the inner sight perceives
subjectively

the eyes define
in separation
the heart intimates
in connection

3/12/15

80. Perceiving Reality

reality cannot be
seen with the eyes
heard with the ears
smelled with the nose
reality must be
felt with the heart

3/12/15

81. Before Dawn

it is in the quiet
moments before dawn
that you can truly
know the world

3/12/15

82. My Lady of Dreams

my lady of dreams
you gave to me my heart
and so my heart is forever yours
my lady of dreams
you remind me of who I am
and so I am forever
defined in relation to you

my lady of dreams
you awoke me from my slumber
and so you are forever
the angel of my awakening

my lady of dreams
no matter what separates us
in waking in my dreams
we remain united

3/12/15

TRANSCENDENT BEAUTY

83. A Delicate Beauty

such delicate beauty
resides within even
the most mundane object
soft and subtle
though it be its vitality
powers all existence

3/12/15

84. Transcendent Divinity

the physical body
is transcended
by the divinity within

3/12/15

85. Death, the Awakening

though it may appear
to be the failure
of the body
death is an awakening
to love a transcendence
of physical limitation an elevation
to a divinity too long denied

3/12/15

86. The Knot of Hatred

the measure of
your hatred is the depth
of your love
thwarted in a knot
of ignorance untie
the knot and free
the love to free yourself

3/12/15

87. Inner Dawn

why does enlightenment retreat
from the dawn
should not the day
be illuminated by
the sun that shines
within

3/12/15

88. Puccini

time stands still
for a Puccini aria

3/12/15

89. A Romance

of all literary themes
it is the love story
that can most clearly
express divinity

in the awakening
of love between
two lovers is captured
the ecstasy and the pathos
of the human condition
and the divinity underlying all

3/12/15

RESONANCE

90. The Resonance of Experience

everything you experience
is a vibration
every every every
thought action object
drawn into your experience
by resonance

91. Synchronicity Is

synchronicity is simply
a conscious awareness
of the operation
of resonance
synchronicity
is applied awareness

3/13/15

92. Wings of Resonance

we fly
on wings of resonance
by resonance we live
and through resonance
do we achieve
our greatest triumphs
and our direst tragedies
in resonance do we
forever sing
of who we are and what
what the world is

3/13/15

93. The Song of Existence

resonance
is

3/13/15

94. Degree of Resonance

resonance is the degree
of affinity
or disparity
between you and your
higher self

3/13/15

95. Experience

experience
is the expression
of resonance

3/13/15

96. Resonance in This Moment

your resonance
in this moment
is your experience
in the next

3/13/15

97. Resonance and Circumstance

your resonance
in this moment is
what matters all else
is circumstance

3/13/15

98. The Magnet

resonance is
the magnet
of probable
reality

3/13/15

99. Resonating Love

breathe from the heart
to resonate love
brings a sun fully
to illuminate

3/13/15

100. Ascension

in clear resonance
of love
you can ascend
to your divinity

3/13/15

REALLY?

101. What Reality

that which we call
reality
is composed of infinite
probabilities

3/13/21

102. Permeability

the seeming permanence
of reality
is a resistance

of the mind to the true
fluidity of
reality

3/13/15

103. The Radius of Action

new dimensions
of whole
reality every birthing
your act outward
slightest radiates
thought
births universes

3/13/15

104. Will the Real You Please Stand Up

all are you
the real
actuality yous
the unchosen in achieving probable each bleeds
path is infinite through to
chosen elsewhere in every in every inspire the other
reference point moment
all substantial all
are every one and vital are
you one

3/13/15

105. The Peacock's Tail

we are the peacock's
tail eyes
of infinite
each I perception
birthing with each
probable eyes

3/13/15

106. To Grasp the Sun

in extending
my arm I reach
radiating infinite probabilities
to grasp the sun

3/13/15

107. The Composite You

who you are
existences is who you become radiating from each
of all probable simultaneous moment-point send love
the composite you to warm
and illuminate

3/13/15

108. Multidimensional Form

every child knows
two mirrors reflecting
in each other an infinity of mirrors
becomes an expression are we reflecting
of infinity into multiples
of infinity each mirror
a reality defining
its own being each mirror casting
through freedom images to reflect
of choice in other mirror
realities
the entire infinite who we truly are
multidimensional flood experience is
of expression and

3/13/15

SPECTRUM

109. My Embrace

my outstretched arms of multiverses
encompass an infinity

3/13/15

110. The Spectrum of the Atom

the atom exists
in a spectrum
of vibration of which
we only perceive
the portion expressed
in our physical existence

3/14/15

111. The Spectrum of Matter

the world of matter
has many expressions
of which we only
perceive this one

3/14/15

112. The Spectrum of Existence

we exist across
a spectrum
of probabilities
of which our waking
consciousness
is unaware only
in our dreams do we
catch a glimpse
of these other realities

3/14/15

113. Tentative Reality

in our dreams we are
open to all tentative
realities of which
this one is the most
tentative

3/14/15

114. The Spectrum of Love

love flows
through all spectrums
it is the connective
force and the impetus
of all existence
love is
the harmonizing influence
that binds all apparently
disparate threads
of existence
together

3/14/15

115. What Common Threads

what common
threads tie together
the fiber of probabilities
the fabric of probabilities
is woven with threads
of love and commonality
woven in such
a pattern that each
fiber compliments
the others adding
strength to the
entire fabric

3/14/15

MULTIDIMENSIONAL

116. Multidimensional Self

sitting here allowing
my awareness to flow
on beams of love I become
a being
of a thousand arms
and ten thousand eyes
sitting quietly in place
in this moment I
become multidimensional
with a hand
and an eye in
each probable actuality
of infinity I became that
which I have always been

3/14/15

117. Multidimensional Dance

my multidimensional Self dances
a dance of infinite
existence infinite
change each step
and every movement
is an expression of
ecstasy and love

3/14/15

118. The Voice of Love

even though we sing
with anger hatred
fear envy greed
sorrow and sadness
these distorted nuances
are sung with
the voice of love

3/14/15

119. The Dawn of My Multidimensional Self

I stand at the dawn
not of the multidimensional
self which is eternal
not even of my awareness
of my multidimensional
nature but of
my understanding
and appreciation
of my awareness and of
my multidimensional self

3/14/15

120. Freedom of Expression

my multidimensional
form is the full
though ever-expanding
expression of
my divinity

3/14/15

121. The Expression of Divinity

the expression
of my divinity
is the recognition
of divinity within
everything and my
acknowledgement that I
am all and all
is me

3/14/15

WHAT MATTERS

122. Thoughtforms

every thought is
an eternal
living world
unto itself

3/14/15

123. Every Myth

every devil and demon
in which you believe
is real for you
and also every god
every myth is real
to those who believe
every heaven and each
hell even unto
the myths of
modern science

3/14/15

124. No Exception

in the infinity
of existence
nothing
is excluded

3/15/15

125. Divine Judgement

the divine
never judges
it revels
in all expression

3/15/15

126. A Matter of Perspective

good and bad
is the judgement
of men and even
among them is entirely
a matter of perspective

3/15/15

BETTER KNOWN

127. All Acts and Probabilities

through our every
act and in
its blossom
of probabilities
divinity
better knows itself

3/15/15

128. Edicts

edicts
are of men
never of
the divine

3/15/15

129. Guidance

if guidance you
seek open
your heart
to divinity
walk always
in the light
of love

3/15/15

130. Dreams United

in my dreams all is
united the living
and the dead
and all probabilities
in my dreams all
veils are parted only
to be drawn by
the light of day

3/15/15

131. Nurturing

in the love of
the divine
all things
come to fruition

3/15/15

132. Cathedral

even this arena of
singular limitations
is a cathedral
of the divine

3/15/15

TRANSCENDENCE

133. Free Bird

the free of heart and free
of mind
can never be
imprisoned

3/15/15

34. Luminous Grounds

looking around me I see
diamonds and stars
in a luminous brilliance
of light and color
these walls that would
restrain
are pathways of
illumination

3/15/15

135. Infinite Greetings

my multidimensional
self is the hand
with which I greet
infinity

3/15/15

136. Every Breath

let every breath
and each perception be
a blessing
then will your existence
be blessed

3/15/15

137. Cloak of Many Colors

even the most
threadbare clothing
is a raiment
divine

3/15/15

138. Transform Yourself

transform yourself
and you transform the world
love yourself
and you open all the world to love
awaken to the divine
within yourself and all the world
will sing of its divinity

3/15/15

139. The World of Perception

the world of our
perception is the translation
of the raw vibrational data
into a form that will
have meaning for us

3/15/15

140. Uncharted Lands

there are charts
of alternative realities
written in light and awareness these are read by
the inner senses interpreted
by the heart and imagination
guided by these charts
intuition can sail
the seas of infinity
bearing home
the riches of
uncharted lands

3/15/15

INFINITE PATH

141. The Paths of Infinity

you travel the paths
of infinity
only in your
multidimensional form

3/15/15

142. In Deepest Sleep

in deepest sleep
you are unbound
traveling freely
in multidimensional form

3/15/15

143. Multidimensional Artworks

in sleep we build
crystalline cathedrals
of loving magnificence
crossing through multiple
realities in the physical
world we encounter but
a glimpse of these edifices
in a breathtaking
landscape a work
of art or a drama
of spiritual
intensity yet from
these works we draw
insight and inspiration

3/15/15

RAPTOR

144. Raptor

large raptor
gliding powerfully
over the mountain valley
in you I see a manifestation
of free flight

3/15/15

145. Rainbow Connection

between
my love
and I
us connected there is
ever keeping a rainbow
of love

3/15/15

146. The Raptor Manifest

the freedom of
the multidimensional
self to span realities is manifest
in the powerful raptor
soaring over the valley

3/15/15

147. Community Confirmation

raptor and vale
have their reality
distinct yet connected and through their connection
their reality bears
confirmation of my own

3/15/15

148. Wink and a Nod

the raptor over the valley
is a synchronicity
through which my
multidimensional self
winks an eye at me

3/15/15

WINTERTIDE

149. The Twinkle of Significance

in the inner and
outward illumination
of all that exists
each twinkle has
added significance for it
holds an added
impetus and acts
as a doorway communicating
between all realities

3/15/15

150. Winter Slumber

the snows of
winter transform
the mundane world
into a crystalline
fairyland
that conducts
awareness
into an insulating
blanket of sleep
under which
the world dreams
itself into being

3/15/15

151. No Precedent

the snows of winter
are followed by the rains
of spring
as night is followed
by the dawn
why then would
we think death
is not followed
by rebirth
the ancients knew better

3/16/15

152. Night Visits

the dead greet us
each night in
our sleep standing
in their perfected
form they offer
comfort love
and reassurance
whispering to us
truths to which we are
oblivious by day
wake up sweet
dreamer wake up

3/16/15

EMOTIONAL ENVIRONMENT

153. Emotional Environment

we live in an unseen
environment
of thoughtform and
and emotions
which can affect
us just as much
as our physical surroundings

3/16/15

154. Anger Within

picking up anger
and aggression
from the emotional
environment is not
it resonant
to aggression
within me

3/16/15

155. Transforming Anger

now I must seek
to transform
my anger transcending
it into love

3/16/15

156. Anger is Energy

anger is the expression
of the energy
for change thwarted
by obstruction
underneath is a desire
to right a wrong
and be recognized
for your true worth

3/16/15

157. What Your Emotions Say

let your emotions speak
to you telling
you what hidden
resonances you
harbor and then
meditate on love

3/16/15

158. Open Your Heart

you have a choice
to open your heart
or close it off
if you are not
doing the first
then you are
doing the last

3/16/15

159. You Live in Resonance

resonate with the violence and you
will live in a violent world
resonate with fear and you will
live in a fearful world
resonate with love and you
will live in a loving world
you live with each according
to the degree of your resonance

3/16/156

FALSE PRIDE

160. The Pitfall of Pride

pride is a reaction
to insecurity
pride is a pitfall
that will leave you injured
on the rocks below

3/16/15

161. Words of Pride

are these words but
an illustration
of my own pride
and vanity

3/16/15

162. Spiritual Pride

to be spiritually proud
shows how truly
lacking you are
in spirituality

3/16/15

163. To Harm Another

to do harm to another
is to injure you both
and to diminish the word
in your disharmony

3/16/15

TRANSMUTED

164. Lessons Learned

to truly learn your lesson
you must let go of who you were
and allow your resonance to reflect
who you are becoming

3/16/15

165. Transmute Emotions

open your heart and allow
love to transmute your baser
emotions then will you
213become spiritually ennobled

3/16/15

166. Bless the Offenders

bless both
those you have offended
and those who offend you
for they have shown you
what base emotions
you must transmute
to raise your resonance

3/16/15

167. Contrast of Resonance

each time I raise
my resonance the contrast
makes more obvious the anchors
that still hold me down

3/16/15

168. Egocentric Relations

once again what others
think of you is not
about you it is
about them conversely
what you think about
others is not about them
it is about you

3/16/15

169. In Joy All Things

in joy
all things are brighter
all matter lighter
all time immediate
and the spirit
free to shine

3/16/15

SYMBOLISM

170. Symbols

symbols are outward
expressions of feelings
for which language
is inadequate

3/16/15

171. Pure Experience

in the pure experience
of the soul all
symbols fall away
and the eternal truth behind
our feelings is known
beyond the capability
of outward expression

3/16/15

172. Divine Truth

the divine truth is
untranslatable in
the outward world
of form
the outward world
in all forms and
probabilities is
the outward translation
of divine truth

3/16/15

173. Eternal Interpretation

as the divine
truth is eternal
and infinite
so is its translation
into outward form

3/16/15

174. Physical Symbols

physical objects
are the symbols expressing
basic feeling tones
of existence
they are
the symbolism
made flesh

3/16/15

175. Your World

your perception of
your physical environment
is your own personal
interpretation of
your resonance with
the basic feeling-tones
of existence

3/16/15

176. Living Symbols

all symbols are living
expressions of the divine
birthing whole new
realms of existence
through their interpretation

3/16/15

177. Shades and Hues

symbols are the paint
on an artist's palette
that change their application
with every canvas

3/16/15

IMPRISONED SMILE

178. The Smile of Ecstasy

ecstasy is a smile
of joy felt throughout
even into your toes
your entire body
down to the least
atom of existence   ecstasy resounds
throughout your spirit
to the very depths
of your soul
and from there
it reverberates through
the entire universe

3/16/15

179. Even in Prison

even in a prison cell
there is a poetry
of wonder   and a love
that breathes infinity
into life

3/16/15

180. Operatic Dreaming

dreaming in operatic
intensity I cast
the die of
living experience

3/17/15

181. Bursting Out

balmy blustery spring
morning burgeoning
with joyous anticipation
and creative inspiration

3/17/15

182. Driven

creative inspiration
drives me into
awakening to
multidimensional reality

3/17/15

GOOD MORN

183. Awakening Sky

the overcast
sky is heavy
with the intensity
of awakening

3/17/15

184. Morning Birth

morning is pregnant
with the living
symbolism of
the coming day

3/17/15

SYMBOLOGY

185. Symbology

everything we see
everything we
know and touch
everything we
are is a living
symbol of our
divine reality

3/17/15

186. Directly

direct experience
stripped of all
symbolism is
beyond reckoning

3/17/15

187. Directly from My Heart

directly from my
heart to yours
is the shortcut
to divinity

3/17/15

MUSIC THEORY

188. The Music of Existence

beyond the range
of human hearing
is the music of existence
it is perceived only
by the inner senses
and the heart

3/17/15

189. The Heart It Sings

the heart it sings
the feeling tones
of existence
make it a song of
unconditional love

3/17/15

190. Find the Song

with intuition
and empathy you can find
the feeling-tone of everything
that exists

3/17/15

191. Harmonize

harmonize your feeling-
tone in love with All
That Exists and the universe
will smile on you

3/17/15

LOCOMOTION

192. The Principle of Locomotion

in empathy feel
the song of anything
that exists
in any time and space
any probability
by intuition and
intent find the wave
form that when married
with your feeling-tone
will produce the song
of that which you seek
let go and resound
and you will find yourself
in this other time and space
or probability

3/17/15

193. Motive Force

love
can take you
wherever
you wish to go

3/17/15

194. The Secret of Locomotion

to go where
you wish first
accept where
you are

3/17/15

195. To Have It All

let go of everything
fill yourself with love
and harmony
for all that exists
now you have everything

3/17/15

196. The Feeling-Tone of Divinity

the song of all
that exists is
the feeling-tone
of divinity

3/17/15

197. In Singing

in singing
the feeling-tone
of divinity
All That Is
is born in
every eternal
moment of existence

3/17/15

198. In Song

in song
is the world
proclaimed

3/17/15

199. Song to Ourselves

we sing ourselves
breath into being
every in every
moment in

3/17/15

200. Beyond All Words

beyond all words
and symbols the song
of existence is known
in the heart

3/17/15

NOTHING MUNDANE

201. Wherever You Seek

wherever you seek
the divine
you will find it
therefore seek
the divine in everything

3/17/15

202. Even the Mundane and Vain

even the most mundane
object and the most
vain of humans sings
a song divine

3/17/15

203. Be Not Tone Deaf

let not ego deafen
you to the song
of all existence truly
it is all that you can hear

3/17/15

204. Profound Mundane

even the most mundane
object sings
a song sublime
and profound

3/17/15

205. To Seek the Divine

if you seek
the divine then look
within finding the divine
within yourself you will
see it everywhere

3/17/15

206. The Grand Chorus

when your heart resounds
with your feeling-tone
you will hear it echoed
in the grand chorus
of all that exists

3/17/15

207. In this Timeless Moment

all particles
of existence
sing eternal
in this timeless moment

3/18/15

THRESHOLDS

208. Death Reaches Not

death reaches not
for us we reach
for death as for
a great awakening

3/18/15

209. On the Threshold

I stand now on
the threshold of
a dream the threshold
of a death the threshold
of a life

3/18/15

210. The Expanse of Existence

in this moment I
awaken from this narrow
dream into the limitless
expanse of my existence

3/18/15

211. I am a Chorus

I am a chorus singing
singing unison singing
harmony within my
feeling-tones you hear
the symphony of my
body organs atoms cells   the prism of my
personality ever changing
the endless harmonies   in its facets
of my probabilities
producing a tonal swath   the multiple themes
of my multiple
and beneath   incarnations
it all the grand
orchestral panorama
of all that does exist

3/18/15

CIRCUMSTANCES

212. In This Moment would You Sing

in this moment would you sing
a song of tragedy or
of glory for myself I prefer
a song of love and divine inspiration

3/18/15

213. No Tragedy

there is no tragedy no
failure, no defeat but by
your perception of them
circumstances are neutral

3/18/15

214. Circumstances Are

circumstances are
what you make of them
even the most dire circumstances
are an expression of the divine

3/18/15

215. Assigned Worth

events have what worth
you assign them
any poverty is born
of your perspective

3/18/15

HIDDEN TREASURE

216. You Can Draw

you can draw blood
from stone gold
from lead lemon juice
from an onion if
that is your perspective

3/18/15

217. Mining Riches

every moment of experience
holds untold riches
it is for you
to mine it

3/18/15

218. Modest Claims

he who lays
claim to
nothing has
everything

3/18/15

219. Riches

he who gives
freely
is rich

3/18/15

220. The Universe Bows

the universe bows
to he who
has an open
heart

3/18/15

221. The Wealthiest Man

the wealthiest
of men is he
who can love
truly

3/18/15

222. The Measure of Wealth

true wealth is not measured
in gold or possessions
but in the depth of
compassion and openness of heart

3/18/15

TAKE HEART

223. No Closed Doors

no doors
are closed
to an open
heart

3/18/15

224. Heart and Imagination

you are free
to the degree
your heart is open
and your imagination unfettered

3/18/15

225. Heart and Mind

your heart
can take you
anywhere to which
your mind is open

3/18/19

226. Journeys of the Heart

in loving resonance
of the heart
there are no limits
to where you can travel

3/18/15

227. Already There

where your heart
and awareness lies
some portion of you
is already there

3/18/15

228. Where Your Heart Goes

wherever your awareness goes
go you to the degree
that your heart goes
with it

3/18/15

FLOWING

229. Fractal Existence

resonate in love
with all that exists
and you extend yourself
to all of existence

3/18/15

230. The Banks of the River

all that exists is a river
of energy flowing
through a framework
of expectations

3/19/15

231. Atomic Flow

each atom is a school
of dolphins leaping
through hoops of physical
form for no purpose other
than the pleasure of expression

3/19/15

232. Free Flowing

energy flows freely
through all of existence
any attempts to constrain it
is a miscomprehension
resulting in a blockage

3/19/15

233. The Flow of Personality

personality is a flow
of awareness through
an architectural framework
of expectations and beliefs

3/19/15

234. The Intersection of Self

the self is not the framework
of expectations nor
the flow of energy but
their intersection

3/19/15

235. The Rise of the Individual

out of the eternal
intersection of energy
and expectation does
our individual existence arise

3/19/15

236. Dawn Greeter

each new moment is
a fresh dawn of existence
what matters is
how you greet the dawn

3/19/15

237. Kindred Awareness

one flow of awareness through
the intersection of this
moment makes of us
all kin everything
that exists in this
moment rides the same
flow of awareness

3/19/15

238. A Singular Flow

the same blood flows
through all our veins
the same air flows
through all our lungs

3/19/15

EXPECTATION & JUDGEMENT

239. The Right of Expectation

grant to all the right
to their own expectation
acknowledge but do not adopt
them as your own

3/19/15

240. Environmental Awareness

be aware of your
environment yet
be aware also
of your reaction

3/19/15

241. Reactionary Judgment

the environment in neither
good nor bad that is
a judgment contained
in your reaction to it

3/19/15

242. No Judgment but Acceptance

make no judgments and none
will be made
accept each moment
in unconditional love and
your expectations will be met

3/19/15

243. Way Station

we have stopped here
a moment so that
you might reassess
take measure
and note how
your expectations
are distributed
now that you are
balanced our journey
will resume

3/19/15

244. The Light of Expectation

expectation is a light
and a song of attraction
a sympathetic pattern
of energy for the flow
of energy to follow
it is not an attempt to constrain
or dam the stream

3/19/15

245. Expectations Are

all beliefs
all thoughts
all feelings
are expectations

3/19/15

246. Predisposed

expectations are
a personal predisposition
that provides a framework
for the flow of energy
and awareness

3/19/15

247. Performance Art

your expectations are an harmonic
or disharmonic structure
built over the foundation
of your feeling-tones
the flow of energy
and awareness is the act
of interpreting this score
into a melody

3/19/15

LIFE IS NOT BIOLOGY

248. The Meaning of Life

the meaning of life
is not the linear
logical interpretation
you impose upon it
it is the experience
of the expression
of the flow
of existence through
the framework of
expectations

3/19/15

249. The Purpose of Life

the meaning of life
is the expression
and acceptance
of love

3/19/15

250. Definition of Love

the recognition
of the divine
within another
and the voluntary
acknowledgment
of relationship
namaste

3/19/15

THE HEART OF THE MATTER

251. Definition of Divinity

the unnamable
undefinable
seed at the heart
of all existence
the one
the all
all is one and
one is all
the holographic reflection
of all contained
within even
the least part
of the one

3/19/15

252. the Moment of the Heart

step into the moment
of the heart
slightly detached
from the world around you
yet open to all that exists
in this moment point

here you can explore
your body
your mind
your feelings
determining
what is in harmony and where
any changes need
to be made

to change is as simple as adjusting
the song or feeling-tone
or flooding
a shadow with light

from here
you can step sideways
exploring the probable moments
linked to this one
here you can test choices
exploring
their reflection in
your body
mind
and feelings
that you can choose which course
you would most like
to pursue in the wakeaday

***

another step
sideways
brings you
to the realm of mass probabilities
where the pulse
of mass migrations can be measured

back to the moment
of the heart
one step
deeper
opens the world of other
incarnations
where by body mind and
feeling you can find
and change those themes
of many lifetimes
and one step
deeper is
the community of this entire
planet here
you merge with forests
continents
you swim the oceans
and explore
the currents and composition
of the Earth itself
all of these
are but baby steps
in the infinite
moment of the heart

3/19/15

253. The Road to Freedom

the road to freedom is found
within this moment
and your experience
of it whether you react
to circumstances
or recognize them as
the neutral camouflage
behind which lies hidden
the divinity of All That Is
then through your
heart lies
the true road
to freedom

3/19/15

STATES OF CONSCIOUSNESS

254. Beyond Our Dreams

beyond the dreams
of wakeaday
connections are
reestablished
All That Is
communes freely
where All is One
further beyond
lie open realms
beyond our
understanding where
if you will strip
yourself and dive
you will surface
bearing the riches
of deep inspiration

3/20/15

255. Altered States

achieved without drugs
altered states are not
altered they are
a clearing and
an opening to who
and what you
really are

3/20/15

256. Open-Minded

as it turns away
from the physical
consciousness strips
away all limitations
becoming that which
it truly is
resplendent in
the attributes
of soul

3/20/15

257. Turning To

in turning away
from wakeaday
you turn towards
the eternal sun

3/20/15

258. Our Task

it is our task in
this life to awaken
and then shine our
eternal sun on the wakeaday

3/20/15

259. Manifest

what you see
outside is but
a manifestation
of what is within

3/20/15

260. Glimmers of Light

through keyholes and
cracks does the light
leak through yet the light
shines out through everything

3/20/15

261. See the Light

when you can see
the light within
you will see it radiate
from everything

3/20/15

262. Seeing is Believing

whatever you see
within will be
interpreted through
your beliefs whether
you see bars
or open doors
whether you bear
anchors or wings
of flight you see
what you believe

3/20/15

263. Abandon Ship

if you would see
clearly abandon all
belief in anything
but love

3/20/15

THERE AND BACK AGAIN

264. Back to Fundamentals

once again we return
to this central exercise breathe
into your heart and radiate
love to all that exists

3/20/15

265. Expectations

do you enter
the unexplored
cave seeking
dragons and riches
do you seek
adventure or do
you seek yourself

3/20/15

266. White Rabbit

symbols of deeper
consciousness sometimes
percolate into
your waking world
only to be ignored
next time follow
them like Alice
follow the white
rabbit into
the hole

3/20/15

267. Symbols Flow

symbols are not cut
in stone symbols are
dynamic and fluid
symbols change and
symbols flow
otherwise
symbols die

3/20/15

THE PERSPECTIVE OF TRUTH

268. No Truth

from our limited
perspective there
are no truths but
subject to change
do you wish to nail
down the truth then
you crucify it

3/20/15

269. Subjective Truth

the truth is
subjective and
entirey a matter
of perspective

3/20/15

270. The Truth Revealed

but first
what do
you want
it to be

3/20/15

271. Seeing around Corners

our senses and
mentality are geared
to the perception of
physical reality
if you would see
anything beyond
then look out of
the corner of your eye
to the perception of
only form
the corner
of your mind
shut the eyes
tune out the mind
feel with the heart
see with the imagination

3/20/15

272. True Sight

looking around corners
you can see simultaneously
what occupies a space
a century past and
a decade hence
you can see an amalgam
of several probabilities
you can see several
faces superimposed and all
of them are true

3/20/15

273. Many Faces

I see in my father
the trusted associate
of centuries past
and the child I
will someday love
he bears the face
of many men
and many women
and every face
is familiar to me

3/20/15

274. Conscious Pretense

consciousness only pretends
to bow to time in reality
it plays with time
it waltzes stepping
into future
past and
present as suits
its whimsy
drawing seemingly
disparate elements
of existence together
by novel lines
of association
to appreciate all
that is from perspectives
unimagined before

3/20/15

275. Unimaginable

the unimagined is
eternally known
in the moment
we imagined it

3/20/15

276. Dream True

in dreams we perceive
unfettered by
the root assumptions
of narrow wakeaday

3/20/15

A TIME OF BIRTH

277. The Beginning of Spring

spring equinox
a super moon
and a solar eclipse
in this time of beginnings
the moon is ripe
birthing its inner sun
so we move into
the manifestation of
our inner suns
radiating through
the camouflage
to bring to light
the underworld

3/20/15

278. Inner Glow

what is that glow
it is the light
of the underworld
peeking through the camouflage

3/20/15

279. Season of the Witch

in this season
of spring let us
manifest our own
awakening

3/20/15

280. Season of Change

with this changing
of the seasons we
proclaim a newborn
world of freedom and love

3/20/15

THE SPIRIT OF THE MATTER

281. No Longer Ignored

even in wakeaday
we no longer can
ignore the spirit
of the matter

3/20/15

282. One Beyond Limitation

the spirit of
the matter is
the one beyond
limitation and at
the heart of it all
the heart of the one
is love

3/20/15

283. Multiplication and Division

by the divine laws
of chaos and
complexity from
the one is born
the all and from
awakening to love
the all are united
as one

3/20/15

284. The Snows of Spring

the snows of spring
bear the crystalline
matrix of the subconscious
into the growing awareness of summer

3/20/15

285. What Lies Within

in opening the heart
to the glow of love
you find the universal
expression of All That Is lies
incubated within

3/20/15

286. The Tiniest Heart

even the smallest
atom had an impetus
to self-discovery
enlightenment bears awareness
of the universe reflected within

3/20/15

287. Positive Feedback

the universe
of within
is a reflection is a reflection
without of the
universe

3/20/15

INFINITE CENTER

288. The Center of the Universe

at the center
of the universe
without and within
is love

3/20/15

289. The Center of Infinity

wherever you stand
is the center
of the universe
open yourself
to love and
you will know this
to be true

3/20/15

290. Relative to You

the center of
infinity is
infinite
therefore the center
is found in every
moment point and within
each atom of existence

3/20/15

291. Center Yourself

find your center
and you find the center
of all existence and there
you find light and love

3/20/15

BIRTHING LIGHT

292. In Enlightenment

in enlightenment you are
the sun birthing
the universe
in light and awareness

3/20/15

293. Birth of the Universe

the universe is born
in each moment
of selfless
self-reflection

3/20/15

294. Emissary of the Underworld

forest cloaked new snow
in a fresh coat falling thick
of white on and silent
the first day of spring raven
wings past from the underworld
finding its way

3/20/15

WHAT DO WE SEE

295. Preferential Awareness

we are aware only
of what
we are
aware

3/20/15

296. Blink

you blink your eyes
twenty times
per minute in each blink
your eyes see
only darkness
yet in your mind
the perception reality itself
so is it any is continuous blinks
surprise your off and on
consciousness blinks one million
blinks
all motion all frames of existence
continuity all of the flickering
linearity in composite
is an illusion built

3/20/15

297. To Each His Own

every path
is valid
for the one
walking it

3/21/15

298. No Longer Your Song

if a song no longer
sings to you
let it go and
find another

3/21/15

299. In the Silence

in the silence
lies infinite
potential
in the darkness
lies the wraith
of our
existence

3/21/15

300. Moments of Conception

it is in the moments
unobserved by
waking consciousness
that we do conceive
everything we
do perceive

3/21/15

QUANTUM EXISTENCE

301. The Quantum Mechanics of Existence I

as the atom exists
as a particle only
in the moment
it is perceived
so we exist
in the world we
perceive
only in
the moment of
our perception

3/21/15

302. The Quantum Mechanics of Existence II

in the moments not
perceived lies
the greater part
of our being
here exists our
universal form
of probabilities
and incarnation
both future
present and past
linked intimately
with everything
that exists

3/21/15

303. Where Magic Occurs

in the moments outside
our perception
is where all
magic occurs

3/21/15

304. The Product of Magic

that which we call
our reality is
the product of
the magic that
occurs outside
of our conscious
awareness

3/21/15

305. Improvised Melody

each note we play
is chosen among
an infinity
of notes assessed
in a suspension
of consciousness right
before we play the note

3/21/15

306. Extension of Consciousness

rather than a suspension
of consciousness
it is a raising and
spreading of awareness
feeling out all
choices at once
to find the choice
that speaks to you

3/21/15

307. Slight of Consciousness

it is a suspension not
of consciousness but
of conscious determination
allowing awareness to
simultaneously feel
out all possibilities
until by intuition
a recommendation
is expressed presented
to ego as choice

3/21/15

GOOD NIGHT

308. Verdant Night

the nighttime is
the most fecund
portion of
the day

3/21/15

309. Fruit of the Night

is it any wonder
that night is the time
of conception
and of birth

3/21/15

310. Night Explorer

my explorations
of the night
are hidden even
to me all I know
are the dreaming
interpretations
of my waking mind

3/21/15

311. Into the Night

the depth to which
you venture into
the night are determined
by how thoroughly
you release
the symbols and beliefs
of the day

3/21/15

312. Who I Truly Am

the boundless opening
of probabilities
and infinite potential and the wakening
focus on this physically
actualized moment

3/21/15

313. Always a Step Beyond

whoever I may perceive
that I am in the next
blink of an eye
I must choose again

3/21/15

314. Stepping Beyond

by the time I am aware
of the step that I
have taken my other foot
is already in midstep

3/21/15

315. The Travels of Ego Consciousness

ego consciousness is aware
not of each step
taken but of
the overall journey

3/21/15

316. Readers and Writers

the reader perceives
the story told
the writer
perceives the words

3/21/15

317. The Space Between

the space between
the words says
more than all
the words ever written

3/21/15

318. The Words Not Said

all of the words not said
are contained
in the space
between the words

3/21/15

THE SPACE OF PERCEPTION

319. Empty Space

there is no such thing
as empty space
the space between two
objects is alive
with infinite
objects not perceived

3/21/15

320. Real Objects

the objects that do not
occupy space are
every bit as real
as those that do

3/21/15

321. Validity

perception is no criteria
for validity
everything you see now was once
only potential

3/21/15

322. Perceived Reality

that which
we perceive as reality
is the choice
made by expectations
from the universe
of infinite potential

3/21/15

323. Real Potential

the quantum field
of infinite potential
is every bit
as real as the world of our perception
in fact it is
from the quantum field our world
is born

3/21/15

324. Born of Dreams

the dream world
precedes
the wakeaday
our world
is born of dreams

3/21/15

325. In a Dream

the world is
born
in a dream

3/21/15

326. We Truly Are

that which we are
is but one expression
of the infinite probabilities
that we truly are

3/21/15

327. By the Grace

by the grace of infinite
probabilities we find
our validity and
our divinity

3/21/15

328. Infinite Existence

the infinite probabilities
of our true existence
extend beyond all boundaries
to encompass All That Is

3/21/15

329. Expanding Consciousness

all potentialities
of any given act are real and are perceived
whether consciously
or subconsciously the choice is yours
but to awaken
to the choices is to grow more fully into who
you truly are

3/21/15

330. Cast Wide

as you can gaze
unfocused on a landscape to take in
the entire scene
so you can cast
your awareness unfocused over
the probable landscape
of any act perceiving
the entire scene

3/21/15

331. The Net of Awareness

cast wide your net
knowing it will catch
only the quarry
you seek

3/21/15

332. Tunnel Vision

you perceive more
when you stop looking
exclusively at what
is in front of your eyes

3/21/15

INFORMED

333. In Pure Form

in its pure
form everything is
a body of light yet
this body of light
is a symbol as are
all forms

3/22/15

334. All Forms

all forms are
symbols through which
awareness
expresses itself

3/22/15

335. All Expressions

all expressions of
awareness are
in their nature
expressions of
the divine as
all awareness is
of itself divine

3/22/15

ARCHETYPES

336. Archetypal Symbols

fundamental symbols shared
by many minds are
archetypes they hold great
potential which can be
tapped for focusing
upon them but cannot disturb
those who do not believe

3/22/15

337. Not to Worship

archetypes are to be
respected but not
worshipped they exist
to serve us

3/22/15

338. Not Gods

they are not gods
but an expression
of the divine
in man

3/22/15

339. Vengeful Gods

if in your mind
you believe the god
archetypes are more
powerful than you
then you had
best not toy
with them

3/22/15

340. No Trespass

there is no trespass
but through
the boundaries
of your own beliefs

3/22/15

341. The Cloud of Potential

each human
and everything that is exists
in a cloud
of potential
here are found
all possible actions of future
past and present
and all other manifested
incarnations
this cloud is the multidimensional
form it is
the action wave of existence and
the manifestation
of freedom in personal expression

3/22/15

342. The Company You Keep

the gods with which you
interact
are an expression of your belief
complexes
and your understanding of the universe
be careful
which gods you choose

3/22/15

THE RICH EARTH

343. Song of the Earth

as everything is composed
of energy
which is itself an expression
of awareness
so the Earth possesses its own gestalt
of awareness
and through this dynamic gestalt
sounds
the feeling-tones of the Earth
all awareness
follows the trend of self
awakening
expanding understanding of the divinity
within
and in so doing expands its own awareness
and potential
and so the Earth is ever awakening
expanding
its awareness in an act we could call
ascension
now all that exists upon the Earth shares in
the base tone
of the Earth in each moment of their
existence
and as the feeling-tone of the Earth
modulates
so must theirs' or they will be caught in
the turbulence
of resistance to eventually change or be
left behind
know that the modulation of change in
the Earth
the modulation of ascension is ever towards
greater recognition
of divinity within the light of divine

love
therefore send your roots deep into
the Earth
and hold your heart open to love and you
will grow
in the light of divinity as the Earth
itself
expands in its awakening we will all be
borne up together

3/22/15

344. The Light Within the Earth

there is a light shining
within the Earth it is
the dawn awakening us
to divinity

3/22/15

345. Star Children

we are star children born
of the stars
each atom has the impetus
to shine

3/22/15

346. Seeking the Sun

as each plant seeks
the sun so it is natural
for us to seek the light
of divinity

3/22/15

347. Expand Within

the greatest expansion
is found in
seeking the light
within

3/22/15

348. Dance with the Earth

open your heart
shine with the light
of love and dance
the earth into awakening

3/22/15

349. Shining Through

the awakening of
the earth shines even
through rusty metal and
the litter of
nonbiodegradable plastic

3/22/15

DANCING FLAME

350. Internal Revelation

and through its internal
illumination
all is revealed to be
angelic
forms of light dancing
in divinity

3/22/15

351. Candle Flame

each candle flame is a dancing
light-form
of revealed divinity
and yes
it is a symbol and an entity
shining
in the light of its
awareness

3/22/15

352. Dance with the Candle

send your awareness
to dance
with the candle flame and in
its light
you will find awakening

3/22/15

TO BE ABORNING

353. Divine Birth

every moment of
existence
is a dawning brighter in
the light
of each moment when it
is born
with an awareness of
divinity

3/22/15

354. Perfection

perfection
is not a state
of completion
but a state
of becoming

3/22/15

355. Happy Birthday

in divinity each
eternal moment
is eternally
born

3/22/15

356. Divine Dawn

in the softness
of this morning
sun let us
find the undefinable

3/22/15

357. The Nature of Action

each action births
an expanding
universe of
possibilities

3/22/15

358. Under Construction

All That Is
is always creating
and expanding upon
itself the least portion
is an I opening
onto infinity

3/22/15

359. All That Is

infinite expansion
of infinite action
simultaneous without
beginning or end

3/22/15

THE FURTHEST EXTENT

360. All

all we
are is all
that is

3/22/15

361. Farthest Extent

at your farthest internal
and external extent you are
infinite and at the heart
of you is All That Is

3/22/15

362. The Turn of the Wheel

see now how the wheel
turns
you are one expression of All
That Is
growing into awareness of your
infinite extent

3/22/15

363. Living Model

the universe is
the model of
the universe

3/22/15

364. Fractal Existence

in seeking yourself
everywhere
you look you find
yourself
everywhere you look
you find
divinity

3/22/15

365. Fractal Form

each least portion
of All That Is
is a full and infinite
expression
of All That Is

3/22/15

SELF-EXPRESSION

366. The Creative Act

releasing the pen releasing
my mind
I relax my focus allowing
consciousness
to range free excited by
inspiration
I take up the pen and focus
my mind
on the words the symbols the
expression
transferring it to the page
I release
the pen release my mind

3/22/15

367. Direct Paths

laughter
not at the expense of another
love
when it is unconditional
inspiration
when it is divinely guided
art and music
when they are an expression of the divine
sex
when it is conducted in love and mutual trust and intimacy
are direct paths
to the sublime

3/22/15

368. Heaven and Hell

to separate to
shut out to
isolate to
cut off this
is hell
to be connected to be
attuned to be
in harmony with
this is heaven

3/22/15

369. In Direct Proportion

the degree to which
you are miserable
is the proportion to which
you make the world
a miserable place
the degree to which
you are joyous
is the proportion to which
you make the world
a joyous place

3/22/15

370. Lighting the World

with love
you make
the world
to shine

3/22/15

BON VOYAGE

371. We Sail with the Tide

the same wind fills
all our sails

3/23/15

372. Purity

the purity
of your purpose
will be the purity
of your experience

3/23/15

373. One Sun

we return now
from the dreams
of sleep into the
wakeaday
yet the sun that our dreams
lights the day that warms
is the sun

3/23/15

374. Balance

let the dreams of day
not keep you from
the sleep of night

3/23/15

375. Shining through All

the first ray
of dawn
illuminates
all that exists

3/23/15

376. Illuminating Gifts

the sun illuminates
every gift
the night
does bring

3/23/15

377. Disclosure

in sleep our gifts
are many the sun
discloses which
we choose to keep

3/23/15

378. Complimentary Dreams

our dreams bear
us nothing with
which we do
not resonate

3/23/15

REFLECTION

379. Reflection

try though you might
you will not see me

3/23/15

380. What You See

all you see is
the reflection of
your own love or
the distortion thereof

3/23/15

381. What Matters

the heart
of the matter
is a matter
of the heart

3/23/15

ANNOYING

382. Go Beyond Discomfort

let the level of
your discomfort
not be the limit
of your love

3/23/15

383. Target Practice

let the source
of your annoyance
be the target
of your love

3/23/15

384. The Source of Annoyance

whatever the outward
appearance the
source of the annoyance
is always within

3/23/15

385. Phase Modulator

let all annoyances
be transformed by
harmonizing love
and acceptance

3/23/15

386. Arbitrary Units

stretch your arms as far as
they will go
call one hand the beginning and the other
the end
this makes as much sense as
anything

3/23/15

387. Predestined

we are predestined
to follow a pattern
that changes at
our every step

3/23/15

388. Dynamics

each breath and
every step
alters the
entire universe

3/23/15

389. The Key to Infinity

within the simultaneous actions
of each eternal moment-
point lies the key
to infinity

3/23/15

390. The Door to Infinity

armed with the key
to infinity your existence
in this moment-point
is the door

3/23/15

391. The Foundation of Reality

the divinity of
all existence
is the foundation
of all reality

3/23/15

392. Dream Foundation

the foundation of physical
existence
is a dream

3/23/15

393. Misdirection

illness and suffering
are the misdirection
of creative energy
clamoring for
a correction
in your state
of being

3/23/15

394. War

war is a glaring
misdirection
of inhumane
ignorance

3/23/15

395. Inexpressible

in existence we strive
to express that
which can never be
fully expressed

3/23/15

396. Training Ground

this physical existence
is a training ground
where we learn to express
our inexhaustible creative energy

3/23/15

397. Traffic Jam

misdirected creative
energy creates a snarl
that leads us back
to inner questions

3/23/15

398. Emanations

everything perceived is
an emanation
of the consciousness
perceiving it

3/23/15

399. Divine Creation

reality is an
emanation
from awareness of awareness
emanates
all potential

3/23/15

400. Mass Hallucination

all events are
emanations of
consciousness without
physical mass

3/23/15

401. Atmospheric Conditions

emanations of consciousness
form an atmosphere
creating the weather conditions
experienced as events

3/23/15

402. Dream Velocity

in our dreams
consciousness can
and does escape
the speed of light

3/23/15

403. Incipient Reality

there is no such thing as a closed
system
everything is permeated by the quantum
field
of incipient reality

3/23/15

DAILY PRAYERS

404. Morning Prayer

we begin again the daily
cycle
drawing from the implicate from
spirit
to manifest in the physical
world
let this day be a true
awakening
bringing with it more awareness
and appreciation
of the source of which this day is but
an expression
may I walk this day in a sacred
manner
making every action a fruition
of love

3/24/15

405. Nightly Prayer

this night I return to my source for
renewal
unfolding the wings of my multidimensional
self
to explore my greater reality within
the akasha
in my sleep may I work out all of
the detrimental
tangles that have been wrought this
day
in the nurturing waters of the dream
world
may I find health abundance love and
joy of heart
may I be a divine light illuminating the
spirit world

3/24/15

406. Daily Dedication

in open heart
I dedicate
this day to
true awakening

3/24/15

407. Daily Intent

let every moment
of this day be
a recognition of
the divine in everything

3/24/15

408. Daily Blessing

in love I bless everything
with which I interact
and all aspects and incarnations
of my multidimensional self
may you be illuminated by
the divine light within

3/24/15

MENDING

409. Fragments

we are each
of us a fragment
striving to become
whole

3/24/15

410. Wholes

we are each
an infinite whole
striving to fit ourselves
into limitations

3/24/15

INFINITE REACH

411. Sending Out

you send your
energy to manifest
in an infinity
of forms

3/24/15

412. Floating to the Top

consciousness always finds
its own level

3/24/15

413. Conscious Property

consciousness has
the property of
maintaining individuality
while seeking to
participate in aggregates

3/24/15

414. Change is Constant

existence without
change cannot
exist

3/24/15

415. Energy Palette

we exist in an energy
palette to which
all entities contribute

3/24/15

EVOLVED

416. Consciousness Creates Form

consciousness spawns
form and form
evolves as
consciousness changes

3/24/15

417. Simultaneous Existence

all consciousness
exists at once
how then could
it evolve

3/24/15

418. Consciousness Awakens

consciousness does not
evolve it simply
comes more
into its own

3/24/15

419. Consciousness Becomes

consciousness becomes
more conscious
consciousness
awakens

3/24/15

420. Expanding Focus

all consciousness is
and in your existence
you experience it as
you expand your narrow focus

3/24/15

421. Consciousness in the Morning Rain

infinite consciousness conceived
infinite forms eternally
evolving in complexity
and then rained down
into these dynamic forms
to manifest them as reality

3/24/15

422. Preexisting

consciousness existed first
and of its experience
formed matter
this is
there is no first
in itself
nor following
a misleading
in simultaneous
statement
time
there is consciousness
expressing itself
as reality in all
forms and probabilities

3/24/15

423. Unevolved

matter does not evolve
consciousness
it evolves itself
in the expression
of consciousness
which is its source

3/24/15

WITHOUT LIMIT

424. No Deities

there is no personified
deity but
the divinity within
all existence

3/24/15

425. You Are a Flux

you are a flux and focal
point
the divine energy of All That Is
which is awareness
pours into you and is emanated
by you
forming its own manifest
reflection
as you form yours

3/24/15

426. No Clockwise Progression

present forms are not based
upon past ones
the future is not born
of the present
future
past
present
are all born point
within this eternal moment

3/24/15

427. In the Moment

all of
incarnations infinite
probable existence
futures moment extends
probable point in all
pasts directions
probable probable
presents

3/24/15

428. The Limits of Selfhood

all limits
to the concept
of self
are arbitrary
limits placed
upon yourself
you are all
that exists

3/24/15

INFINITE IDENTITY

429. Who Are You

are you the air
you hold in your lungs
are you the water
you drink every day
are you the food
you eat in every meal
are you the atoms
of your body, flickering wave-particles of energy
are you the interstitial space
between the comparatively minute subatomic particles
are you the quantum field
that permeates all space
are you the flow
of consciousness manifesting in form
you are the universe
you are All That Is
individuating
to discover itself
within its self-expression

3/24/15

430. Everything Is

everything is
a flow
of spirit
through form

3/25/15

431. Open Yourself

open yourself
to the flow
of the divine
and it will wash
away all blockages
and distortions
open yourself
to the flow
in all things
and you will
find harmonious
resonance
in all

3/25/15

432. Ego and False Pride

ego is simply
the interface between
self and the world
all else is false pride

3/25/15

ETERNAL SEASONS

433. The Seasons Flow

the seasons flow
with each heartbeat
and in every
breath

3/25/15

434. The Seasons of Consciousness

the seasons are
a cycle within
the consciousness
of everything that exists

3/25/15

435. No Time

it is not time
that orders events
but our linear
perception

3/25/15

436. Beyond Our Perception

all beginnings and endings are only
apparent
they mark the movement of
events
into dimensions outside of our
perception

3/25/15

437. Interface

the I of self that most
perceive
is more truly the
interface
between
the inner self and
the outer world

3/25/15

438. Transition Zones

it is in the transition
zones
that you find the greatest
focus
and variety
of expression they
are
dynamic interfaces where
consciousness
abounds in complexity

3/25/15

439. Skin Deep

the skin is truly the organ
of the ego
as the skin is the interface
between
you and the world

3/25/15

440. Identity Crisis

you should not
identify
so closely with
your ego
would you identify
only
with your skin

3/25/15

NEEDLESS INTERCESSION

441. No Worship

rather than worshipping
deities it is
better to open
yourself to divinity

3/25/15

442. Dial Direct

what need is there
for intermediaries
when you have a direct
connection to the spirit
that flows
through all
things

3/25/15

443. Metaphor

everything that exists
is
a metaphor
existence
is
a metaphor
I
am
a metaphor

3/25/15

444. Spirit Helpers

all spirit helpers all
guardian angels
are an extension of self into a
separate
yet connected entity
if you think
that this statement
belittles
their validity then you
belittle yours

3/25/15

445. Flatland

events are multidimensional
realities
infinite and eternal that can
never
be fully perceived in our
limited
dimensions of space and time

3/25/15

446. Self-Expression

the whole self
is a multidimensional
entity that can never
be fully manifest in
our three-dimensional
reality

3/25/15

447. No Time at All

seconds and moments are
but a three-dimensional
perception of phenomena
that form the multidimensional
aggregate that we perceive
as time

3/25/15

448. In Moments Beyond

in dreams and in moments beyond
consciousness
blinking moments in every second of
existence
of which we are unaware
we express the multidimensional
reality
that cannot be experienced in three-dimensional
wakeaday

3/25/15

BEYOND DENIAL

449. Sleep Deprivation

denied sleep and dreaming
multi-dimensional
existence will flood into the
wakeaday
misinterpreted as hallucinations
and insanity

3/25/15

450. That Which Cannot Be Denied

sleep deprivation is a denial
of your greater
multidimensional
existence

3/25/15

451. Confinement

the only walls are those
you build
yourself move beyond
those walls
and you are free

3/25/15

452. Self-Expression

there are no boundaries to
the self
we spend eternity exploring
our own
existence and in so doing
discover
all that exists

3/25/15

BE ALL YOU CAN BE

453. Capacity

every atom has the capacity
to become
a universe

3/25/15

454. Beneath the Surface

beneath the surface
lie
infinite possibilities

3/25/15

455. Beyond the Flowering

beyond the flowering
of your three-dimensional reality in this moment
is the flowering
of all probabilities related to this physical moment
beyond the flowering
of all immediate probabilities
is the flowering
of all simultaneous moments
beyond the flowering
of all probable simultaneous moments
is the flowering
of all incarnations and associative probabilities
beyond the flowering
of all associative probable incarnations
is the flowering
of the whole multidimensional self in communion
beyond the flowering
of the multidimensional entity
is the flowering
of all gestalts in communion upon this Earth
beyond the flowering
of this planetary gestalt
is the flowering
of all conscious existence
beyond the flowering
of all that exists
is the flowering
of all extradimensional pyramid gestalt entities
beyond the flowering
of all pyramidal gestalt entities
is the flowering
of the One within All That Is
beyond the flowering

3/25/15

456. Boundaries Only

these walls are the
boundaries only
of my physical perception

3/25/15

DREAM HOUSE

457. Dream House

the house of my dreams
holds innumerable
sunlit rooms inviting
the weary traveler
to rest and dream
communicates through
endless corridors
lined with statuary
of the multidimensional self
contains
throughout
are stands
of houseplants
libraries art rooms
meditation rooms
music rooms play rooms
private studies
the walls
are covered in
paintings and tapestries

the kitchen
is a house unto
itself with walk-in
pantries freezers
and a greenhouse garden

the bedrooms
are soft and inviting
as clouds of
floating dreams

the yard is a garden
and a playground
and a place of exploration
and communion

outbuildings include
a craft shop and a greenhouse
of rare and tropical plants

the back gate
opens into
a forest

3/25/15

458. In My House

in my house
of dreams
all rooms are events whether
dreams or
probabilities
all windows and doors
open to unexplored
expanses
and all halls
lead into
infinity

3/25/15

459. The Walls of My House

in my house
all the walls are built
of thoughtforms
and experiences
and every room
is illuminated
by love

3/25/15

460. Floor Plan

the floor plan
of my house
is a mandala an ever-changing
heart mosaic of
leads to the rooms and
passage hallways
turns every where for all
the twists and

3/25/15

461. Visitation

I saw you in my dreams last night
you looked so vibrant glowing
with health so full
of life so full
of love and joy

I felt you in my dreams last night
I hugged you as I kissed
your head you were so
solid so much bigger
than life so extant

I spoke to you in my dreams last night
and you just smiled
and told me that
you loved me

It was no dream I saw you in
aglow with spirit
though you were aglow
with life you reassured
me that you were
truly there

3/26/15

462. My Dreams Reverberate

the emotional intensity
of my dreams reverberates
through my body and through
my waking consciousness
they are as valid
as any psychological event
of the wakeaday

3/26/15

463. The Greater Reality

my thoughts my
emotions my
expectations steer
my life they truly
direct the manifestation
of my waking
existence they possess
the greater reality

3/26/15

464. The Message from Beyond

I am as real as you
stay the course
but most of all
you are loved
and keep playing
that music

3/26/15

SHAMAN, POET, LOVER

465. The Flow of Ink

when my pen touches
paper my
consciousness
touches the divine

3/26/15

466. Seeing Beyond

so long as you continue
telling the story
of reality as you
understand it
you will not be long fooled
by the camouflage

3/26/15

467. Telling the Story

telling the story
in the end always brings
me back to the fact
that it is a story I tell

3/26/15

468. Uttering Truths

the truth as soon
as it is uttered
is no longer
the truth

3/26/15

469. The Complete Truth

the truth is never
complete
it is always being
discovered

3/26/15

470. My Love Holds

my love holds a place
wherever
I am I know I have
a place
within her heart

3/26/15

471. A Staircase for My Love

I build
a staircase for my love
a staircase
manifest of love that she might
climb
beyond the moon and stars to take
her place
in the Pleiades of my heart and soul

3/26/15

472. The Debt I Owe

the debt I owe you is as deep
as my own soul
you were there for me even when
I was not there
for myself

3/26/15

473. You Led Me to Myself

you believed in me when I believed
in nothing
when I was lost in pain and
abnegation
you took me by the hand and
led me
to the light of my own higher
self

3/26/15

478. I Shower You

I shower you in blooms
of unfettered love
and diamonds of divine
awareness
I lay you on a bed of
tenderest blessings
and deliver kisses directly
to your heart and soul

3/26/15

479. I Know You Always

I recognize you in all
incarnations
you are
the queen of my dreams

3/26/15

480. Beneath It All

beneath all limiting beliefs
and the outward perspective
of denial
every one of us knows that
we are but divine rays
of a sun
that lights our whole reality
and of which we are the most
that can ever
be manifest

3/26/15

481. Beyond Expression

what metaphors we
enact to express
that which can never
be expressed

3/26/15

482. Prime Examples

in our prophets in
our geniuses in
our most sublime
artists we see
expressions of
the divine that exists
within us all

3/26/15

483. The True Message

the true message
of true leaders
geniuses artists and prophets
is not
look at me nor even
follow me
it is
that which I have done
you can do

3/26/15

484. Capability

that of which
one is capable
all too
are capable

3/26/15

485. True Leaders

true leaders show
us our limitations
and how to step
beyond them

3/26/15

486. Lighting the Path

those seers who hold up lamps
in the night
they do not show us
the path
they show us
we are the path

3/26/15

THE RASA LILA

487. Religious Dramas

all religious dramas explore
the theme
of the multidimensional inner self
that can never
be wholly manifest within
three-dimensional
reality

3/26/15

488. Lift Your Eyes

manifest here
the sun would burn us up
to see the sun
you must lift your eyes

3/26/15

489. Radiance

they who consistently lift
their eyes to see
the sun will become
the sun

3/26/15

490. The Premiere

we are attending the premiere
of a new passion play
the actors have not yet
taken the stage

3/26/15

491. Act Two, Scene One

in the next drama to be
enacted
we will all take the
stage
we will each perceive
our own
divine sun and we will all
ascend
in radiance along with our
entire planet
the Earth will raise itself to a higher
dimension
where all of us can more fully
manifest
the brilliance of our true
divinity

3/26/15

492. Intimate Communion

the higher self speaks most clearly
when we are at rest
in meditation
in sleep
there it communicates
in insight
and intuition
speaking to each
according to
their understanding

3/26/15

POWERHOUSE

493. Lift Your Heart

love joy and honoring
the spirit
can overcome any
adversity
transforming even the most
confining
circumstances into the
divine

3/27/15

494. True Power

true power acts with
the lightest
of hands
it has no need to enforce
itself

3/27/15

495. Forgetting Yourself

in failing to honor the spirit
that flows through all things
you forget yourself
in this world we are all
capable of forgetting
ourselves
this is no reason to condemn
yourself make
amends excuse yourself
and pick up where you
faltered

3/27/15

496. Predisposition

it is all decided
by your predisposition
all meaning is assigned
by the perceiver

3/27/15

497. Extant

as your body is
an extension
of the Earth
so is nature an
extenslon
of your being

3/27/15

498. Radio Free Underworld

in the underworld that interior
reality
all communications are known and
understood

3/27/15

499. Talk to the Animals

speak to the trees the birds
the dragonflies
communicating freely what is true
in this moment
meaning is transmitted and understood
on the flow of spirit

3/27/15

500. Dialogue with Nature

you engage in a dialogue
with nature
whether you are listening
or not

3/27/15

501. Nature Hears

nature hears
and responds to everything
you say
whether you vocalize the words
or not
nature hears
and responds to you why do
you not hear
or respond to it

3/27/15

502. Selective Hearing

everything you think
and feel
is broadcast to
all that exists
all intentions are known
only man
deigns not to hear

3/27/15

503. Let's Be Honest

where all is one
of course
all intentions are known
you are
the only one not being honest
with yourself

3/27/15

504. Not Abandoned

it is not nature or spirit
that abandoned
us it is
we who stepped away

3/27/15

505. Standing Apart

it is by our intent that divinity
was externalized
becoming something
separate to us until we could
no longer feel
its existence
now that we have so thoroughly
isolated
our identity
it is time to reawaken the divinity
within

3/27/15

506. Transference and Misappropriation

our own inner reality has
become a thing
not real
perceived only as it is
projected
into the outer world
we have lost the intimacy
and validity
of our own divinity
no wonder then why we try
to fill ourselves
with externalities
seeking to find fulfillment
in possessions

3/27/15

507. Fulfillment

until you find fulfillment
within yourself
you will never be
fulfilled

3/27/15

508. Inner Unity

the universe is created
and perceived
by all that exists in
knowledge
of their inner unity
only man
pretends to stand apart
ignoring
this inner unity

3/27/15

509. The Greater Reality

ignoring
the greater reality
within
we deny
the greater reality
without

3/27/15

510. Burned Bridges

we have burned
all bridges to forge our
independent perspective
yet now we see all bridges
are still intact

3/27/15

511. A Bridge Too Far

who knew that the bridges
we tried to burn
would be those that
lead us home

3/27/15

512. The Ego is a Vengeful God

the reflection of the ego
is a vengeful god
stridently proclaiming
its existence

3/27/15

513. Ego Consciousness

the development of ego
consciousness
added new dimensions
to reality
yet now it is time
to connect
that ego back
to source

3/27/15

514. The Dammed Ego

born from within the ego
erected a dam
between inner and outer
reality
yet always nagged by the
subconscious
knowledge that inner and outer
are one

3/27/15

515. Feedback Loop

ego
is a feedback loop
between inner
and outer reality

3/27/15

516. White Caps

ego rides the crest
of a wave
where ego perceives
the wave to falter
as it reaches shore
the momentum
of the wave is passed
along through mediums
imperceptible from within
the sea

3/27/15

517. Short-Sighted

in its inability to see
beyond
its own borders
the ego fears that
which would
assure it
of its own validity

3/27/15

518. The Ego Fears

the ego fears
its own
immortality

3/27/15

519. Dancing Diaphanous

we are a thin veil
of existence
dancing through the flow
of vital waters

3/27/15

520. Being Redefined

ego is the seed from which
you can be reborn
as that you once were
are and ever
will be
now given greater definition
in your new-found
ego awareness

3/27/15

TRUE HEART

521. The Heart Knows

the heart knows
all truth

3/28/15

522. The Truth Knows

the truth known
to the heart
is not the truth
the eyes perceive
the heart feels
truly
while the eyes
are deceived

3/28/15

523. Neurons of the Heart

the neurons
of the heart
bridge
the universe

3/28/15

524. All Things

all things respond
to love

3/28/15

525. With Every Breath

an open heart
can traverse
the universe and does
with every breath

3/28/15

526. May You Soar

may you soar
with the spirit
that flows through all
things both in
your dreams and in
the wakeaday

3/28/15

527. Looking Out through the Heart

in the transit
of my mind
as it looks out
through my heart
all things are
illuminated

3/28/15

528. Differing Outlooks

the eyes look out
upon the world
the heart looks out
upon the soul

3/28/15

LOST AND FOUND

529. Human Drama

the drama of our search
for ourselves
as the drama of the loss
of ourselves
is by reflection staged
within the world
around us

3/28/15

530. Dramatic Resolution

we have been here
all the time
around us and
within us

3/28/15

531. Hidden in Plain Sight

everywhere you look
hides
that which you seek
stop looking
open your heart and
it will be
revealed

3/28/15

532. Behind All Faces

behind all faces
there is one face
behind all visions
one pair of eyes
behind all thoughts
one mind
behind all feelings
one heart

the one face recognizes
the individuality of all faces
the one pair of eyes sees
the validity of all visions
the one mind enthusiastically follows
the flow of all thoughts
the one heart shines in
the expression of all feelings

3/28/15

533. The Journey of the Gods

the journey of the gods
is the journey
of our own lives
and awareness

3/28/15

534. Awakening the Ego

it is time for the ego to rub its eyes
and awaken
allowing itself to look within as well
as without
in free communication and commerce with
the deeper portions of the self
perceiving as well as the external form
the divinity within

3/28/15

535. The Gods to Which

all gods are projections
that set up
fields of attraction
therefore be careful
to which gods you pray

3/28/15

536. Release Your Gods

release your gods
and free yourself
in the open conception of
All That Is

3/28/15

537. Unlimited Scope

look for the gods and you shall
find them
in dreams of limited scope

look for All That Is and you
shall find it
in All That Is

3/28/15

538. Careful Beliefs

be careful of the beliefs
you accept
for by them you shall know
your world

3/28/15

539. Caught in the Spotlight

shine a light of love joy
and freedom
upon all gods and all beliefs
if they run
from the light
dismiss them

3/28/15

540. Expectations

you perceive only
what you accept
as reality

3/28/15

541. The Devil, You Say

as are the gods so are
all demons
and devils
projections of your
beliefs beware
the demons
with which you do battle

3/28/15

542. Partial Perception

we only perceive a portion
of the whole
and from those slices
knit together
our limited reality
with the thread
of similarities

3/28/15

543. Opposites

opposites are portions
of a whole
we cannot perceive
within our limited dimensions

3/28/15

544. The Whole Truth

how can we claim
to know the truth
when we cannot perceive it
in its entirety

3/28/15

545. Dawning Awareness

now we are at least
becoming aware
of what shall one day
plainly be seen

3/28/15

546. Wholistic Vision

as we elevate our awareness
to a new dimensionality
we shall soon be able to perceive
the wholes of which
this limited reality is composed only
of parts

3/28/15

547. To Perceive the Whole

to perceive the whole of which
this three-dimensional world
is only a part you must
close your eyes
and open your heart

3/28/15

548. The Holistic Organ

the heart is the holistic organ
of multi-dimensional
perception

3/28/15

549. Higher Dimensional Brain

the neurons of the heart
form a higher dimensional
brain that processes
the inner senses

3/28/15

550. The Senses of the Heart

the inner senses are open
to higher dimensional
holistic perception
they are the senses of
the heart

3/28/19

551. Opening Awareness

in order to open ourselves
to higher dimensional
perception we must
grant validity to that which cannot
be seen with the eyes
or heard with the ears
but can only be felt with the heart

3/28/15

552. Greater Validity

the perceptions of the
higher senses
have a validity
that can only be measured
in the heart

3/28/15

553. The Sunshine of Your Love

the greater holistic
reality is
only illuminated
by the heart

3/28/15

554. The Most Acute Sense

the heart responds to music
the ears cannot hear
canvases of hues
the eyes cannot perceive
perfumes the nose
cannot smell
making it the most acute
of senses

3/28/15

555. Perceiving Beyond

the senses five and the brain
are for perceiving
this physical world
of three dimensions
the inner senses
and the heart
are for perceiving what
is beyond

3/28/15

556. Expanding the Field of Vision

by opening the heart
and cleansing
the ego we can achieve
a 360˚
field of vision

3/28/15

557. Visions of the Heart

life reaches out
through the visions
of the heart

3/29/15

558. Heart Seeker

if you seek to know
spirit
look not with your mind but
with your heart

3/29/15

559. The Spirit of Perception

if you would see spirit
look with your heart
not your eyes
if you would hear spirit
listen with your heart
not your ears
if you would know spirit
think not
with your brain
but with your heart

3/29/15

560. Dream Architect

the architect of my dreams
incorporates
its richest sculptures into
the dream
of waking existence

3/29/15

561. Treasures of the Dream World

treasures of
the dream world
attain their greatest
value when realized
in the waking world

3/29/15

562. The Reality of the Dream

the dreams of the waking
attain full value
in the greater dimensions
of sleep

3/29/15

563. Born of Two Worlds

the blossoms of our dreams
give us
the fruit of our waking world

the blossoms of our waking world
give us
the fruit of our dreams

the full cycle of existence
is realized
between the two

3/29/15

564. Sunrise, Sunset

the sunrise of morning
is born
of the dreams of night

the dreams of night
are born
out of the eve of day

3/29/15

565. Multidimensional Awakening

upon awakening to your
multidimensional
existence
you will be surprised at how
rich a life
you have lived
the least thought in this
waking world
gives birth
to entire universes barely sensed
from the limited
perspective
of this waking experience echoed
dimly
in dreams
only in the multidimensional self
can you fully
explore the riches
born of the wakeaday

3/29/15

566. The Library of Probable Books

I sit in the library of probable
literature
and from
the infinite shelves I draw a book
opening the
cover
inside I find an entire universe
might I
check out
a few tomes to take home
for leisurely
perusal

3/29/15

567. Beyond Grasp

the multidimensional self will not be
bounded
defined measured or categorized
it cannot be
cornered caught or caged
any attempt
to grasp it in your hands is destined
to failure
yet your entire life is one thin
expression
of its existence

3/29/15

568. Known with the Heart

the multidimensional self
cannot
be grasped with the hands
or defined
with the mind but it can be
known
with the heart

3/29/15

569. The Act of Creation

there are creative gestalts
pyramidal
compounds of consciousness
that create
beautiful complex patterns
of light
which they then set to singing
working out
their own dimensional
expression
each dynamic edifice of
light
itself blossoming into a
myriad
of creations each portion
a source
of further vital exposition
birthing
infinite and infinitesimal
universes
without end

3/29/15

570. The Laughter of Existence

the creations of the pyramidal
gestalts
are the expressions of their laughter
born
in delight of the joy and love
of existence

3/29/15

571. In the Music of Their Laughter

the pyramidal gestalts are
not gods
though gods they may seem
to us
any conception we may have
of them
falls short of their reality
they are
the super souls that desport
themselves
in the music of their laughter

3/29/15

572. Chasing Our Tails

in the music
of their laughter we chase
our tails around

3/29/15

573. Go Outside and Play

we chase chase chase
knowledge a living spirituality
chase chase chase
a dream desire respect
chase chase chase
pleasure our dinner understanding

better
to go outside
and chase
your tail

3/29/15

574. Touching the Divine

for all our attempts to
understand
and attain
it is in play that we
most truly
touch
the divine

3/29/15

575. Put Down the Book

why
are you still reading
these words when
you should be outside
playing

3/29/15

576. The Product of Laughter

all that exists is a product
of laughter
therefore
all existence
is a garden of delight

3/29/15

577. Laughter

laughter
is a transcendent act
it is the sound
of all potential
all creation
laughter
is the sound
of the universe being born

3/29/15

578. The Comedians

the fool the clown
the trickster
are the most divine
of archetypes

3/29/15

579. The Gift of the Magi

the greatest gift
you can give
to others is
to make them laugh

3/29/15

580. The Light and Song of Existence

love is the light
of existence
and laughter is
its song

3/29/15

581. Laughter and Tears

crying is the other side
of laughter
of the two is the spectrum
of existence
composed without one
the other
would be incomplete

3/29/15

582. The Essence of Tears

the essence of life is distilled
from tears
of laughter and of sorrow

3/29/15

583. My Love Welcomes

my love welcomes
me into my own
heart which has
ever been her home

3/29/15

584. My Love Introduced

I did not find my love
by searching my love
found me and
introduced me to my own heart

3/29/15

585. My Love Revealed

when finally I opened
my eyes
my love
stood revealed before
me where she
had always been
whispering to me in my sleep

3/29/15

586. The Greatest Treasure

the greatest treasures
are those
least valued their worth
is only appreciated
in their absence

3/29/15

587. Blue Skies

the skies so blue
let's jump off
the springboard
and dive right in

3/29/15

588. The Center of Infinity

in an infinite universe
where all
is one
the center is within

3/30/15

589. The Center Is

the center is
the spirit of
divinity
within you
the center is your heart

3/30/15

590. The Center Holds

the center holds
so long as you
stay focused
upon it

3/30/15

591. At the Center

at the center
of your universe
is you at the center
of my universe is me

3/30/15

592. Out of Focus

focus upon
anything else
and the center
will not hold

3/30/15

593. Relative Rotation

hold your focus upon
the center and all things
will revolve around you
focus upon anything else
and you will revolve around it

3/30/15

594. All Tied Up

be not tied up
in events
or they will keep you
tied down

3/30/15

595. Point of Influence

from your center nothing
can displace you but you
have the ability to stir
all else about you

3/30/15

596. Point of Power

in your center within
this moment is your point
of power from here
you touch all that exists

3/30/15

597. Willy-Nilly

lose your focus within
the center of this
present moment and you
are swept willy-nilly

3/30/15

598. Don't Forget

All That Is is centered
within you
in this moment
do not forget it

3/30/15

599. When Long Battered and Bandied

when long battered and bandied
by the storm hold to
this center and eventually
the winds will settle
the sky will clear and
the sun will emerge from the clouds

3/30/15

600. Grounded and Centered

you are not grounded
in the Earth
you are not centered
within ego
you are grounded and centered within
the spirit that flows
through all things
within the One that is the All
here is your grounding
and your center
and here the power behind
all miracles
and magick

3/30/15

601. True Magick

in magick as in
all else
the focus is not on
the desire
the focus is upon
the center within

3/30/15

602. Eyes on the Goal

the focus is the goal
from which
desire is a deflection miracles and manifestations
are to be expected
keep your eyes on the goal

3/30/15

603. Keep Centered

to keep centered
through any hardship
is to find divinity
within

3/30/15

604. Central Sun

centered within
you touch
all that exists

3/30/15

605. Open Center

the center is open
shut yourself off
to your experience in this moment
and you shut yourself
off from your center

3/30/15

606. Shut Off

shutting yourself off
is just another
way to display
your focus

3/30/15

607. No Eclipse

centered you shine equally
in all directions
without any threat
of being eclipsed

3/30/15

608. Twin Suns

each focused on the center
within
we form a positive feedback
loop
thus between us our light
is amplified

3/30/15

609. Reflecting Centers

may looking within my heart
reflect the center
within you as
your heart does for me

3/30/15

610. Out of Reach

when we try to reach
for each other
only then
are we out of reach

3/30/15

611. Extending Touch

extending our light
each to the other
then are we
truly in touch

3/30/15

612. The Truth My Love has Shone

love is
seeing the divinity of All That Is
reflected within the heart of
another and while both maintaining
distinct centers rotating in
harmonic orbit to create a combined
center between the two
this truth my love
has shone to me

3/30/15

613. A Greater Love

the twin rotation of mutual
love creates at the center of
its orbital
the perception of the higher level
reality seen there
so it is the loving
interaction of the electrons
that gives mass to the nucleus
to the atom

3/30/15

614. Born of Love

the human body
the Earth the solar system
the galaxy the universe
all are born
out of love

3/30/15

615. Reinforcing Harmony

maintaining focus
upon your center
of divinity reinforces
the harmony at the center
of All That Is

3/30/15

616. The Magick of the Sun

the magick of the sun
is to shine
in love joy and vitality
never worrying
what it shines upon

3/30/15

617. The Good Driver

the good driver always
keeps his eyes
on the road
stay the course

3/30/15

618. All Answers

to find the answer to all
things look to the center
of your heart there you
will find all things

3/30/15

619. Only Fulfillment

centered within there are no
questions only answers
no desires only
fulfillment

3/30/15

620. Harmonic Sorting

centered within all else
is sorted out
into its appropriate
harmonic position

3/30/15

621. A New Dawn

by the light of your
central sun
a new day
will dawn

3/30/15

622. Given Voice

every word
an expression
every sentence
a new creation
every syllable
a derivation
every letter
a mutation

3/30/15

623. The Central Sun

all of existence
is a glittering
fractal mosaic
in reflection of
the central sun

3/30/15

624. One Center

there is one center
at the center
of me
at the center
of you
at the center
of All That Is

3/30/15

625. The Points of the Compass

all points of
the compass
are found
at the center

3/30/15

626. The Maypole Dance

All That Is within the One
centered
at the heart of me
spins in delight
as all that exists dances round

3/30/15

627. Not Man Apart

your soul stands not apart
it is the most intimate part
it is your breath your
awareness your essence
it is
a divine expression
of All That Is

3/30/15

628. No Separate Gods

there is no need
for separate gods
no god is an island
no god is
no god but the One
that is All That Is
and that one dwells within

3/30/15

629. I'd Rather Dance

why kneel
to a false god
when you can dance
with the god within

3/30/15

630. Vision of One

each moment each atom
of your soul contains of the universe contains
the entire soul the entire universe
centered within
each moment
and every atom
lies the heart
of All That Is
within the infinite
eternal awareness
of
the one

3/30/15

631. Group Portrait

there lies a group portrait
in holographic essence
within the glint
of every eye the beat
of every heart and the light
of all awareness

3/30/15

632. All Parts Rise

all parts of you
are elevated
by the elevation
of any part

3/30/15

633. Reading Light

the light of one
is seen
by all the light
of all
is seen by one

3/30/15

634. The Center of All

within your center
all things
are
centered

3/30/15

635. Galactic Consciousness

there are galactic
consciousnesses
for which the entire
history of our planet
is but one blink
of the eye
and yet they are centered
each
within
you
and
I

3/30/15

636. Singular Consciousness

at the center
of you space
and time are
meaningless
at the center
of you
lies a
singularity

3/30/15

637. The Physicist's Conundrum

the singularity is the scientist's
expression
of the spiritual truth that All
is One
and the One is All and within this
framework
there lies a singularity within the center
of every portion
of existence while there is only one
singularity
upon which all of existence is etched

3/30/15

638. A Singular Observation

in the limits of his own
perception
the physicist overlooks the
implications
outside of our linear experience
of time and space
there are no beginnings nor endings
all exists
at once therefore all that exists
is contained
within one singular singularity

3/30/15

639. The Scientist Cringes

the scientist cringes
from that which
the mystic embraces
and yet his circular
logic will lead him
there in the end

3/30/15

640. The Scientist and the Mystic

the scientist and the mystic
will eventually meet
and there find
a common ground

3/30/15

641. Common Ground

at the seat of the soul
all things meet
and there find
a common ground

3/30/15

642. The Proof is in the Pudding

the purpose of the scientist
is to prove that nothing
exists nor can be proven
except in the subjective reality
of the heart

3/30/15

643. Unacceptable

within its own framework
science can never
accept the proof
it seeks

3/30/15

644. Beyond Our Grasp

the secrets of the universe
lie forever beyond
our grasp until
we look within

3/30/15

645. Degree of Freedom

that which belongs
to you is
that to which
you belong

3/30/15

646. Grasping Freedom

if you would
be free
let go

3/30/15

647. Free Love

love is not
possession
love is freedom
from possessiveness

3/30/15

648. Unfounded

that which you find
outside of yourself
is unfounded that
which you find inside
yourself is true

3/30/15

649. To Look Within

to look within
you must first
release the ego
from false pride

3/30/15

650. Keep It in Your Sights

whether looking inside
or outside
never lose sight
of your center

3/30/15

651. Lantern Light

shadows
loom large
in the brightness
of the lantern

3/31/15

652. Too Revealing

is to say
the tendency too much
by the light
better are revealed
to let others what treasures
discover for themselves

3/31/15

653. Making the Bed

after a busy
night
we make
our beds

3/31/15

654. Sleeping Naked

in the morning
we don clothes
after sleeping
naked

3/31/15

655. Go Naked

we take not even
our bodies
with us into our dreams
yet we are
richly provided for

3/31/15

656. Empty-Handed

you must come
empty-handed everything
you might need or want
will be provided

3/31/15

657. Why Fight It

do you not trust
yourself
you wrestle only
with yourself

3/31/15

658. Avoidance

you avoid only
yourself in the end
you will be met
with love

3/31/15

659. How Obvious

how obvious
the truth must
be that you
avoid it so

3/31/15

660. Misidentification

why make yourself
a flickering shadow
when in truth you are
the lantern light

3/31/15

661. What Glory Holds

what glory holds
the masonry when
you do not force
it to be a wall

3/31/15

662. Tender is the Night

the night reveals
things for what
they truly
are

3/31/15

663. Early Morn

in the dark hours of early
morn while
the world still slumbers
its beauty
is revealed

3/31/15

664. Mining

my mind is busy early
bearing to the surface
the riches unearthed
during the night

3/31/15

665. Each (Encapsulated

each (encapsulated
and expressed
in a breath at
observation) moment

3/31/15

666. Within (Parenthetically

within (parenthetically
hide the truth) form

3/31/15

667. My (Open-Ended

my (open-ended
burst
of sunlight) life

3/31/15

668. The Dawn of (Infinite

the dawn of (infinite
source of
probabilities) the day

3/31/15

669. Outward (Ever-Changing

outward (ever-changing
variegated diamond
of intrinsic
beauty) expression

3/31/15

670. Through (Energy

through (energy
and awareness
eternally
passing) form

3/31/15

671. Moment (Eternally

moment (eternally
and infinitely
encompassing All
That Is) point

3/31/15

672. Exterior (Interior

exterior (interior
center of
divine
creation) manifestation

3/31/15

673. Parenthetically Centered

centered
within (everything
that exists) your
heart

3/31/15

674. A Part of Me

a part of me
is traveling
with you
it is the best part

3/31/15

675. The Six of Us

your perception   my perception
    of me (who   of you (who
        I really am)   you really are)
            (the truth within
                us both)

3/31/15

676. Outer Self (Multidimensional

outer self (multidimensional
resplendent
fractally
blossoming) of limited scope

3/31/15

677. To Know (You Must

to know (you must
look within
the self
you know) yourself

3/31/15

678. Within the Willing Desire (There

within the willing desire (there
must be a willing
acquiescence)
to know yourself

3/31/15

679. Let Us Open (Through the Open

let us open (through the open
window we fly)
the window to let in
(bounding through all
open landscapes) some fresh air

3/31/15

680. Your Soul] Your Soul) Your Soul

no other can direct you to
(only you can find
[All That Is lies within
your soul] your soul) your soul

3/31/15

681. My (Me [Me <Me {Me

my (me [me <me {me
—One is All
All are One—myself}
conceiving> manifesting]
experiencing) experience

3/31/15

682. Oasis (Spring

oasis (spring
of divine
vitality)
of experience

3/31/15

683. Holy Communion

this is my body (spirit flows
through all things
interconnected
yet apart) this is my blood

3/31/15

684. Reality (Framework

reality (framework
of thoughtforms [energy
and awareness
folded {influx
and outflux of
the divine} upon
itself countless
times] empowered by awareness
and expectation) manifest

3/31/15

685. Within My Heart, My Love

within my heart
(I {my love
enfolded within
me} my love)
two are one

3/31/15

686. A Love So Pure

all worlds tremble
at a love so
pure it will
make you cry

4/1/15

687. Such a Love

such a love gives
birth to All
That Is in every
moment of existence

4/1/15

688. Antipode

become an antipode freely
communicating such a love
and all that exists will
quicken to your charge

4/1/15

689. No Rhyme Nor Reason

within such a love there
is no rhyme nor
reason but the expression
of divinity

4/1/15

690. Purpose

your purpose is to
communicate divine love
let all else work
its way for you

4/1/15

691. Give Yourself Over

when you have wholly
given yourself
to divine love
all of existence
will dance to your tune

4/1/15

692. What It's All About

realizing divine
love and giving
yourself over
is what its all about

4/1/15

693. Surrender

surrender
and you will be
given the key
to the kingdom

4/1/15

694. On Purpose

the purpose of
existence is the free
and full expression
of divine love

4/1/15

695. Not About

it is not
about you
it is about
you

4/1/15

696. Degree of Resistance

illumination is measured
in the degree
of resistance
to divine love

4/1/15

697. On the Spectrum

on the spectrum between
ignorance and
divine love lies
the full expression
of all that exists

4/1/15

698. One Eye Opening

the spectrum of existence
is an eye opening
to recognize
itself

4/1/15

699. Third Eye Opening

one eye opening
sees itself
two eyes opening
see the world
third eye opening
sees divinity within

4/1/15

700. The Secret of Divine Love

the secret of divine
love is that it is no
secret except to those
who refuse to see it

4/1/15

701. Tail Chasing

all else is chasing
your own tail
but is not that
a most joyful expression
of the divine

4/1/15

702. The Glory of the Mundane

the glory of the mundane
is found within
its singular expression
of the divine

4/1/15

703. Give All to Love

give all
to love and
all will come
to you

4/1/15

704. The Object of Symbols

the objects of symbols are
physical expressions of
inner experience they are
divine camouflage

4/1/15

705. The Cloaking of Divinity

every inward glimmer
of divinity
is cloaked
in a physical form

4/1/15

706. Chrysalis

it is but a thin shell
to outward
appearance the miracle
takes place within

4/1/15

707. Reality Concerto

reality is
a symbolic
statement produced
in concert

4/1/15

708. Who Do You Think You Are

you are not your
body your physical
form is an expression of
who you think you are

4/1/15

709. The Flow of Symbols

symbols are the expression
of consciousness
as consciousness changes
so do its symbols

4/1/15

710. Translation

to direct change become
versed in your symbolism
and then learn how
to translate it

4/1/15

711. The Language of You

the first step
in self-mastery
is to learn
the language of you

4/1/15

712. Be not Misdirected

train yourself not
to look at
the symbol but at
the inner actuality
of which it is an expression

4/1/15

713. Not Reality

the physical expression
is not reality
do not waste yourself
tilting at windmills

4/1/15

714. Fluidity

you are always in a state
of becoming true
reality is as fluid
as your state of being

4/1/15

715. April Fools

the walls you bang
your head against
will never be
overcome in that way

4/1/15

716. Always the Fool

we are always
fools when we
mistake reality
for its physical expression

4/1/15

717. Divine Fool

the divine fool looks
behind the wall
where most see
only the surface

4/1/15

718. Fluid Dynamics

when focused on the physical
it appears intractable
yet the inner actuality
is always in a flow

4/1/15

719. The Ocean We Perceive

the ocean we perceive
is but one phase
within a cycle if we would know
water we must
perceive it within the flux
and flow of the entire
cycle the ocean is a flux

4/1/15

720. No Criterion

the physical world is not
the criterion of reality
the framework of existence
flows from within

4/1/15

721. Caught Up in the Drama

we are so entranced
we forget
we are the projector
the film
is our beliefs through which
we shine
the light of divine awareness
to project
an image on the screen of
physical existence

4/1/15

722. Changing the Movie

to change the movie
we must change
the reel of film
not the screen

4/1/15

723. No Prisoners Taken

to say you cannot change
reality is
to say you are
a prisoner

4/1/15

724. The Dimension of True Reality

the dimension of true actuality
is experienced
subjectively first as feeling-tones
holistic concentrations
of awareness that flow through
the psychological
landscape and can then be translated
into structures
of light and color from which
are derived
frameworks of thought and beliefs
which themselves
give rise to images of symbolic
import that
then give impetus to physical
manifestation

4/1/15

725. The Webwork of Reality

all events actions and thought complexes
are webworks of focused
energy and intent that communicate
between the lightforms
of all living entities here
is the latticework
of reality within this
moment-point
dynamic and ever-changing
focus upon
the divine love expressed
throughout
this pattern and it will respond
reorganizing
itself in harmony with your
song

4/1/15

726. Which Song You Sing

do not sing the tragic lay
of physical
circumstances
let physical experience resound
with the hymn
of your divine existence

4/1/15

727. The Magick of Transformation

from the inner dimension of feeling-tone
focus upon the circumstance
you wish to alter and
its feeling-tone will become
prominent now from within
this feeling-tone call up the primal
tone of loving divine
awareness and allow it to bring
the feeling-tone of the circumstance
into harmony allow it
to shine freely singing without
any barriers or restrictions
now allow your own relation
to this feeling-tone to change
upon returning to physical
expression allow your
relation to the circumstance
to change and the circumstance
will dance with you

4/1/15

728. One Step Beyond

the greatest truths
lie always
beyond the sphere
of your beliefs

4/2/15

729. Beyond Grasp

I am always reaching
beyond the limit
of my grasp and now
I can lay hold of
what was once
beyond my imagination

4/2/15

730. All for Love

I know I must step
beyond all beliefs and
reasoning if I am
to be with you

4/2/15

731. What I Find There

for love of you
I step beyond
myself yet there
I find us both

4/2/15

732. A Fellow Traveler

a fellow traveler once told me
he was weary of the journey
for all the ground he had covered
he could not take another step
the love and refreshment I offered
was as empty as the air to him
giving him my blessing I continued
on my way
looking back I saw
he was securely
tethered to
the rock upon which
he sat seeing
this I was moved
to look about my own
waist seeking
to find and break
my own chains

4/2/15

733. Reminder

let no other
overshadow
your center hold
to it within

4/2/15

734. Curses and Blessings

with judgment criticism and
complaints
we curse the world and
ourselves
with love appreciation and
acceptance
we bless the world and
ourselves

4/2/15

735. The Acceleration of Inspiration

the acceleration
of inspiration can
move you to an entirely
new reality

4/2/15

736. Grasping What is Beyond

to be deeply moved
by inspiration
is to grasp what is
beyond your reach

4/2/15

737. Inspiration and Creation

inspiration is an act
of opening the mind
yet once the words are
transcribed inspiration
has already stepped beyond

4/2/15

738. Allowed Free Rein

allowed free rein
inspiration
takes us
beyond our reckoning

4/2/15

739. A Merry Chase

inspiration leads us
on a merry chase
yet in this pursuit
we are more fully alive

4/2/15

740. The Chase

the thrill is in the chase
once attained
the goal is quickly
left behind

4/2/15

741. Supposed Vulnerability

how frantically others seek
to cover
their supposed vulnerability
little dreaming
it is the source of all strength
and vitality
their efforts to hide their
own light
endearing though they seem would
be better
to let it shine unhindered

4/2/15

742. The Tastiest Fruits

the tastiest fruits
lie
outside the orchard

4/2/15

743. Rampant Inspiration

true inspiration
is an ivy that runs
rampant soon overtaking
the boundary of the garden

4/2/15

744. Driven

no matter how fast
he runs the artist
is always trailing
behind his inspiration

4/2/15

745. Leaving Port

the scaffolding that supports
the rocket ship
is abandoned once
the rocket takes off

4/2/15

746. Out of Bounds

intuitive knowledge always
oversteps intellectual
frameworks only the fearful
are content to stay within bounds

4/2/15

747. Living Webs

we are living webs of
actuality reaching
far beyond all
we perceive

4/2/15

748. Shine Unconfined

seek to keep your light
confined
within the framework of
your belief
and you will find yourself
confined
the light to your eyes
extinguished

4/2/15

749. Free Egress

the doorways exist
within us all
all it takes is the desire
and confidence to open them

4/2/15

750. Expressions of Truth

a flower is the truth
so is
a lady of refinement and
a flea
upon her neck all are
expressions
of the truth as it is by
them known

4/2/15

751. All Forms

the truth takes
all forms yet
is never fully
known

4/2/15

752. The Living Truth

in encountering the living
truth
the consciousness
expands
this expansion
is the act of grasping
the truth which is
the expanding consciousness

4/2/15

753. Integrity

the integrity of any truth
communicated is found
within the integrity
of the one communicating it

4/2/15

754. Self-Approval

to expand you must
become aware
of the beliefs and
prejudices you seek
to expand beyond

4/2/15

755. Inseparable

you cannot
separate yourself from
your experience
all encounters
with divinity
are in relation
to yourself

4/2/15

756. Self-Discovery

you
are the truth
therefore discover
yourself

4/2/15

757. Every Step Taken

every step
taken in love takes you
closer
to the divinity within
all things
and within yourself

4/2/15

758. Every Blow Struck

every blow struck
in anger
and in hatred
erects another
barrier between
yourself
and your
source
another barrier
you must overcome

4/2/15

759. Karma

karma is an obstruction
created
that must be overcome through your own action
before you can be
united with your source

4/2/15

760. Karma is Erased

karma is erased
through awakening
to self-awareness
and divine love

4/2/15

761. The Light You Shine

what light you shine
upon the least part
of existence you shine
upon yourself

4/2/15

762. Finders Seekers

that which you seek
is here with you
now all that is necessary
is to open yourself to it

4/2/15

763. Step On It

any step taken
by ego alone
is the wrong step

4/2/15

764. Never Say I Am

I am says ego
never looking further
I exist says spirit
seeing all

4/2/15

765. Soar with the Eagles

see by the light
of divinity walk
by its grace and you
will soar with the eagles

4/3/15

766. The Magnificence of the Ego

the magnificence of
the ego lies
in the divine source
it has forgotten

4/3/15

767. Lantern Loss

ego is only the lens
of the lantern
through which divine
light shines

4/3/15

768. Your True Self

your true self
is divine love
in divine love you
are true to yourself

4/3/15

769. The Vastness

the vastness you
do not perceive
is where you have
your true existence

4/3/15

770. Color Blind

you look for only the similarities
that reinforce
your beliefs
if you would see as well the dissimilarities
you would have
some clue
how big the universe really is

4/3/15

771. Perceiving Organization

your thoughts perceive organization
and of that
organization
you build the walls that enclose you

4/3/15

772. Your Conceptions

you only perceive
your own ideas
reality is built
of your conceptions

4/3/15

773. Your Environment

conception proceeds physical
form
you exist in an invisible field
of thoughts
and emotions where your conceptions
are harmonically
aligned with those of all about you

4/3/15

774. Medium of Expression

you transpose your ideas
into reality
the atoms
and molecules are your medium

4/3/15

775. Resonant Matter

it is only when your conceptions
resonate
with the energy particles that you see them
as matter
otherwise you see only the space
that is
ninety percent of the atom

4/3/15

776. A Matter of Convenience

your root assumptions govern
your conception
of reality
and yet they are no more
than an
agreement
a matter of convenience

4/3/15

777. Your Pulse

you are a pulse of your greater
dimensional
existence
as it pulses in resonance with
this physical
your
higher self keeps the beat

4/3/15

778. Heart Beat

your heart is the physical
expression
of the pulse
of your existence
it is the organ
by which you
physically manifest

4/3/15

779. The Heart of the Matter

when your heart stops
beating
your pulse of existence
is no longer
connected to this body

4/3/15

780. The Way to Expansion

there is no way to explore
the greater
dimensions
of reality other than through
the exploration
and expansion
of your own consciousness

4/3/15

781. Inner Exploration

in traveling through your own
consciousness
you discover
all of existence and
your intimate
vital
connection to All That Is

4/3/15

782. Divine Dance

divine and
loving inspiration
compels the dancing of the molecules
the dancing of
all conceptions
all awareness and indeed
the dancing
of your self

4/3/15

783. True Spirituality

true spirituality
is a dance
of divine
inspiration

4/3/15

784. The Teacher at the Heart

there are many teachers
but the one
for you lies
within your own heart
you need only
open the door
and make the introduction

4/3/15

785. The Teachings of the Heart

to hear and abide
the teachings
of the heart
you must first quiet
your mind
and bring
your ego into line

4/3/15

786. Hush

to truly know
your self
you first
must silence your ego

4/3/15

787. Beyond Conception

you must first reject
all definitions
if you would
know yourself

4/3/15

788. The Call to Sun Rise

we cannot call upon
the sun
to rise
the sun will rise if only
we will awaken
ourselves
in time to see it

4/3/15

789. Open Heart, Open Door

open your heart to the spirit
flowing through
all things
and the spirit
flowing through
your heart
will open the door to you

4/3/15

790. Death is My Doorman

death is my doorman and greatest
teacher
in slaying
the dragon of false ego death
opens the door
to the true self
the spirit that flows through all things

4/3/15

791. Heroic Service

the ogre kept the maiden chained
to an enormous
boulder yet
when the hero appeared and broke the chain
all vanished
the ogre
the maiden
the hero and the chain all
that remained
was the spirit
that flows through all things

4/3/15

792. No Teacher

the teacher is no
person
place
thing or
practice
all these are merely vehicles through which
the spirit
that moves
through all
things may act
to achieve awakening

4/3/15

793. A thin Window

ego is but a thin window
of tinted
glass
that seems to separate
inner
and outer
reality yet on both sides
of the window
we find only
the spirit that flows
through
all things

4/3/15

794. Necessity

when the student
is ready
the teacher
will appear

4/3/15

795. Filling the Void

all voids
exist
only to
be filled

4/3/15

796. Already Yours

all you
desire know
it is already
yours

4/4/15

797. Natural State

the enlightenment
you seek is indeed
your most natural
state of being

4/4/15

798. Be Light

do not seek
enlightenment
be light

4/4/15

799. Let It Shine

the light is
already within
you let it
shine

4/4/15

800. Already Known

there are no
questions for which
the answer is not
already known

4/4/15

801. True Spirituality

true spirituality
is a joy
that sings
throughout existence

4/4/15

802. Revere Each Moment

revere each moment
with delight let
consciousness dance to
the song of your heart

4/4/15

803. Merry Abandonment

cherish each
moment in
merry
abandonment

4/4/15

804. Abandonment

to find
your Self
you must abandon
yourself

4/4/15

805. The Bells

the bells are merrily ringing
within each moment
within everything
hear the tolling of the bells

4/4/15

806. The Treasure of the Mystics

true spirituality is of
the Earth and
of the stars
and within the laughter of a baby
true spirituality
is the treasure
within each moment of existence

4/4/15

807. Delighted Weaver

with what delight you have
woven
yourself
within the fabric of time
and space
to create
this tapestry of existence

4/4/15

808. Woven Strands

each moment of time and space
is a vertical
strand through which
you weave your horizontal existence
yet all strands
coexist
now within the fabric

4/4/15

809. Multidimensional Actuality

lay multiple sheets of space/time
fabric atop
each other
and weave across the sheets
know the
entire carpet
is but a single thread

4/4/15

810. Casting a Light

every moment of existence
is eternal
and open-ended
and the light that shines within
each moment
casts its glow
upon all existence

4/4/15

811. Spread the Word

your state of being within this moment
affects all
other moments
past and future and within
all incarnations
and probabilities
what song would you sing with All That Is

4/4/15

812. I am an Infinity

I am an infinity of eyes opening
to see
the light
I am an infinity of ears hearing
the song of
divine existence
I am an infinity of mouths singing

4/4/15

813. Infinite Awakening

infinity is within the grasp
not of your
eyes or mind
but in your heart felt as an infinite
radiance of
divine love
open your heart to infinity

4/4/15

814. Infinite Arms

you are an octopus of infinite
arms reaching
out to tickle
the belly of infinity

4/4/15

815. Divine Loom

with infinite arms
you weave the
multidimensional
warp of your existence

4/4/15

816. Communal Weaving

from your singular point of awareness
you throw out
your threads
and from their singular points all
others throw
out theirs
and of these interwoven threads
the webwork
of reality
is formed

4/4/15

817. Pulsation

permanence is not a property of
physical matter
it is an illusion
of our perception the atoms
pulsate
everything
pulsates on and off from our
perspective
we pulsate on and off
our consciousness
pulsates
on and off so that we are
only aware
of the moments
when we are on composing
of them
our continuous
reality of the moments when
we are off
other we's
compose their worlds
multiple we's
multiple worlds
in the spectrum of infinity

4/4/15

818. In Stillness Feel

in stillness feel
divinity flowing
through awareness
allow this light
to illuminate all action

4/4/15

819. Let Go

let go of all
strictures
circumstances
conjectures
the divinity within
is beyond
all of that

4/4/15

820. A Deeper Pool

fall into a deeper pool
of silence
brimming
with loving divinity

4/4/15

821. Not with the Mind

do not seek to know
the spirit that flows
through all things
with the mind the divine
cannot be
comprehended
with the intellect
it must be
felt within
the heart only through
the heart
can it be
comprehended

4/4/15

822. With the Heart

what cannot be comprehended
with the mind
can be embraced
with the heart

4/4/15

823. The Thinnest Line

I am but the thinnest line
compounded
between
the divinity within
and
the divinity without

4/5/15

824. Crossing the Line

once that line
is crossed
there is
nothing but divinity

4/5/15

825. The Line

the line
itself
is compounded
of divinity

4/5/15

826. The Mystery

the mystery is that the line
is composed
of divinity
and is written upon divinity
how then
can the line
maintain any distinction

4/5/15

827. Endless Iterations

the written words are
composed of divinity
the record of thought
composed by divinity
conceived by mind
composed of divinity
as an expression of the heart
composed of divinity
in its experience of brilliant love
composed of divinity

4/5/15

828. Ocean and Sky

floating on the surface
of the ocean
of divinity
we gaze up at the sky
which is
itself
divinity

4/5/15

829. One Step Beyond

floating here we free
all symbols
from physical
expression so they become
fluid mixed
in the
currents of awareness

4/5/15

830. Back to You

allowed to drift freely
all oceans
and all currents
bring me back to you

4/5/15

831. Hold the Center

it is not the wakeaday
that impedes
but your reaction to it

hold to your center knowing
all else
revolves around it

4/5/15

832. The Senses and the Heart

the senses are great
liers
that keep you engrossed
in the camouflage
yet the heart knows
the truth
within

4/5/15

833. The Secrets Known

the secrets have been known
since before
the earth was the Earth
since before
the stars existed the secrets
were known
they are known intimately
within
your higher self they are
whispered
intimately listen with your heart

4/5/15

834. From Within

within your heart lies
the teacher
whispering
the secrets of all existence
shift your
awareness from
the camouflage
and you will be shown how
it is
in fact
you create your own reality

4/5/15

835. Covering Your Eyes

what
so you do not wish to know
yourself
and master
the universe then go back to worshipping
your gods
and let them
run your life

4/5/15

836. Fear Not Yourself

there is nothing to be
frightened of
but yourself
all that exists and
the demons
and gods
of your own design

4/5/15

837. Demons and Gods

the demons and gods
are naught
but a figment
of your own deluded mind
dismiss them
open your heart
to the truth of divine love

4/5/15

838. Self-Mastery

your higher Self is
a microcosm
of the spirit
that flows through All
That Is
master yourself
and you master All
That Is
become your
Self and you become
All That Is

4/5/15

839. Ecstatic Abandonment

dance with your Self
to the pulsation
of consciousness
and matter
then will you
become yourself
in a dance
of ecstatic abandonment

4/5/15

840. Walking Dead

you are deader now than you
will ever be
in sleep and in dying you are
more fully alive

4/5/15

841. The Embrace of Death

let go of the coffin
you clutch
to your chest
and you will become alive

4/5/15

842. This Earthly Plain

truly death embraces us now
upon this earthly
plain and when at last he loses
his grip then
we come alive

4/5/15

843. To Die and Be Reborn

to evade the grasp
of death
is to die
and be reborn
to the divinity
within
all of existence

4/5/15

844. Easter Sunday

on this Easter Sunday
let us
stage an uprising
let us
roll away the stone

4/5/15

845. Within This Dream

when you wake within
this dream
you wake
into your whole self

4/5/15

846. Let the Fun Begin

once you awaken
within this dream
the adventure
truly begins

4/5/15

847. Awakening from Sleep

you who have been asleep
since being born
are now awakening
step out
and greet the sun

4/5/15

848. Born Alive

you are born alive
then lulled
to sleep
and now must awaken
to become
once more
alive

4/5/15

849. Too Narrow a Definition

living in the wakeaday
in too narrow
a definition
of the noun life

4/5/15

850. Become Alive

life truly encompasses
dimensions
and realities
few experience from
their waking
perspective
we must become alive

4/5/15

851. Claim Your Birthright

living is the
birthright
we have been
denied

4/5/15

852. Innate Majesty

innate majesty comes
from within
ego senses this yet fails
to see
the source of this majesty is
the divinity within
and so over-compensates with
false pride

4/5/15

853. Certainty and Insecurity

false pride is born
of insecurity
majesty is born
of the certainty of inner divinity

4/5/15

854. Majesty Expressed

majesty is not expressed
by lording
it over others
majesty is expressed
by shining
with the light
of divine love

4/5/15

855. No Right

majesty is not a right
to rule
but an awareness
of the divinity within all

4/5/15

856. The Veil of Fear

the veil between
the individual
and higher Self
is composed of fear that
in the higher Self
the individual
will be lost this fear
is born of
the ignorance
of ego which understands
not that it
is maintained
by and of the higher Self

4/5/15

857. Intrepidation

show courage in the face
of fear
and you will come home
to your Self
and gain the universe

4/5/15

858. Fear of Hatching

should the baby chick
or butterfly
give in to the fear
of hatching
then it will die within
the shell

4/5/15

859. Couched Environments

the physical environment is but
a reflection
of the psychic environment
if the psychic
environment is lit by the sun
of divinity
the physical environment will
glow brighter

4/5/15

860. Focus on the Center

focus on the physical and you live
within the body
focus on the inner center and you live
within the divine Self

4/5/15

861. Footsteps of Giants

we all walk in the footsteps
of giants
where most see only the rim
of the print
those who look up will see
legs rising above

4/5/15

862. Magnetic Patterns

when centered within
your heart
it will sound with a resonance
to which all else
will eventually be oriented

4/5/15

863. Guided by the Heart

keep your heart centered
upon divine
love
and eventually your mind
will be entrained
to the divine Self

4/5/15

864. Original Sin

there is only one sin
that to close
your eyes to
the divinity within you
and in all things
this is the original sin
the only sin
ignorance
behind all transgressions
and when your
eyes are cleansed of this sin
your heart
will open
to all divinity within
you and
within all that exists

4/5/15

865. Imbibing Poison

when others curse you they
are generating poison
you do not have to
drink it but they
surely do

4/5/15

866. This Prison

this prison is a holy
sanctuary
where I find
enlightenment

4/5/15

867. The Prison I Inhabit

at least I can see
the prison
I inhabit
and know it for the blessed
delusion
that it is
how much worse for
those outside
who cannot see
the prison walls around them

4/5/15

868. Moving On

having manifest
the prison
I can now
manifest my freedom

4/5/15

869. No Prison

where the heart
is open
to divinity
there is no prison

4/5/15

870. Run with the Spirit

the open heart runs
with the spirit
that flows
through all things

4/6/15

871. Temple in the Heart

there is a temple
in the heart
that is
inviolate

4/6/15

872. Ego Bows

in the temple
of the heart
ego bows
before the divine

4/6/15

873. The Eternal Flame

in this temple
burns the eternal
flame of the
infinite source

4/6/15

874. Open Temple

this temple touches
all dimensions
yet occupies neither
space nor time

4/6/15

875. The Fountain

around the flame
there is a fountain
of awareness pouring
continuously

4/6/15

876. Enter to Hear

enter this temple
barefoot to
hear the word
of your higher Self

4/6/15

877. All Is Hallowed Within

all is hallowed within
this temple and everywhere
its light shines through
its light shines everywhere

4/6/15

878. Follow the Tolling

to find this temple
you must follow
the tolling
of the bell

4/6/15

879. Once You Enter

once you enter the temple
you will discover
you have dwelt
within it always

4/6/15

880. Nothing to Attain

there is nothing to attain you are
already divine
you meditate to purify the mind
raising
the vibration of awareness
so that
it is open to the divine

4/6/15

881. Release All Ballast

the divine is within
you always to rise
to its level
release all ballast

4/6/15

882. Subtle Nature

the divine is of a subtle
nature
often outshouted by physical
existence
though its voice sings through all

4/6/15

883. Consciousness is not Imprisoned

consciousness is not imprisoned within
the body
it dances
through all that exists within this
moment
it pulses
in and out extending itself into all
probabilities
all dimensions
only ego places its boundary
at the skin
the only thing
that holds you back is you

4/6/15

884. Consciousness Perceives

even without eyes ears nose
mouth
and skin
consciousness perceives and
perceives
more clearly
through the senses of the heart

4/6/15

885. An Awareness that Perceives

there is within everything
an awareness
that perceives
with creative abandonment

4/6/15

886. Song of Joy

all that exists the very
air and every
thought sings
the joy of its existence

4/6/15

887. Atomic Celebration

the atoms sing
and dance
themselves
into existence

4/6/15

888. Expanding Universe

in the dispersion
and extension
of awareness
the universe expands

4/6/15

889. Seeing Truly

until you have unburdened
your self
everything
and everyone is a projection
of your fears
and prejudices
until you free yourself
to the divinity
within
you cannot see truly

4/6/15

890. Truly Known

everything you think and feel
is sensed
by all
and understood all of your fears
and prejudices
are seen
but known as the curtain of
your ego
underneath
is perceived the love and
compassion
that is
truly you

4/6/15

891. Projector

you project your thoughts
and feelings
outward
into the world your
subconscious
is broadcast
to become manifest

4/6/15

892. The Deeper Current

do not worry over the thoughts and
feelings of which
you are ashamed
your worry only strengthens them
beneath lies
a stronger current
of love and divinity focus here

4/6/15

893. Here not There

focus here not
there
at the heart
lies the divinity
that is
your truest
identity

4/6/15

894. Building Walls

whenever you hide your feelings
from yourself
you build walls
you must then demolish

4/6/15

895. Less Alive

each time you close yourself
off to your
thoughts and feelings
you are less alive

4/6/15

896. Entombed

when you have finally entombed
yourself
the only thing
that can break through is anger

4/6/15

897. The Anger of the Entombed

for those who are entombed
anger and
aggression
are a vital breath of air

4/6/15

898. Communicating Feelings

communicate your feelings
if only to
yourself
in expression they will be transformed

4/6/15

899. The Same Spirit Lives

the same spirit lives within
and without
the spirit is awareness
and the outward
expression of awareness is matter

4/6/15

900. Pleasure Seekers

the pleasure we seek
in all outward
stimulus
can only be found within

4/6/15

901. Our Precious Illusions

all of our precious illusions
are only a pale
reflection of
the divinity within

4/6/15

902. I Am That

this body the breath flowing through
the water
the food
the excrement excreted
the flesh and bones the perception
of the senses the beating of the heart
I am that

the clothes I wear the table where
I sit the walls the electric lights
all who live and work here
I am that

the sun in the blue sky the breeze
the trees the birds and insects
the earth and the grass
I am that

the sun and moon the planets and
the galaxies this expanding universe
the atoms and molecules the elements
the wave/particles of the subatomic realm
I am that

all thoughts and feelings that flow through
my awareness my beliefs and symbols
my dreams and my subconscious my ego
and my id and something undefined
I am that

***

the awareness of my mind and
consciousness the light and love
radiating from my heart above all
the concentrated gem of divinity and
the spirit that flows through all things
I am that

an ecstatic dance of creative
awareness the song that awakens
all that exists and the divine
love that radiates through all
I am that

4/6/15

903. Transitory Nature

all things
are transitory but the spirit
that flows
through all things and in
that spirit
you reside

4/6/15

904. The Voice of the Spirit

in this moment
of existence
you are the voice
of the spirit
that flows through all things
you are its eyes
and consciousness its
expression of existence
in this moment

4/6/15

905. The Bird that Sings

the bird that is lost
within its own existence
sings a feeble tune
the bird that sings
with the spirit
that flows through
all things sings true

/6/15

906. True Communion

everything you eat
drink or breath
is a manifestation
of the divine

4/6/15

907. Don't Give Up

you would not give up
on the sunrise
do not give up on
enlightenment
it will come just as surely

4/6/15

908. The Flow of Divinity

inhale
the spirit that flows
through all things
exhale
your individual awareness
of divinity

4/6/15

909. Energizing Ecstasy

in the spirit that flows
through all things
is the ecstasy
that energizes all

4/6/15

910. Only This Joy

let go of everything that holds
you back from ecstasy
of divine love
only this joy is real

4/6/15

911. Divine Ecstasy

divine ecstasy will take you
to the infinity of the universe
or the infinitesimal atom
to higher dimensions
and probabilities
there is nowhere you cannot go

4/6/15

912. Stick Shift

in a trance we sit oblivious
to the miracle
of our own existence
we do not even have to shift our trance
but only allow
ourselves the freedom
to change our focus
to see what else
exists just beyond
the periphery of our vision

4/6/15

913. Persecution

you cannot be persecuted
by demons
past lives
black magic
or childhood trauma
unless you believe
in the nature of
your fear and allow
yourself to be persecuted

4/6/15

914. Realize It

you free yourself
from any prison
simply by realizing
that you are free

4/6/15

915. Peeling the Onion

what beliefs whether conscious
or subconscious
stand in your way
realize they are limitations
and all limitations
are false
what other beliefs
still stand
in your way
peel away the layers of
false belief
know you are
divinity unbound

4/6/15

916. What Do You Want

you get exactly what
it is you want
therefore embrace
the divinity within you

4/6/15

917. Every Act Counts

every act changes
all of reality
let go your fictions
of determinism and continuity
let go of all
limiting beliefs
and reach for your divine self

4/6/15

918. Holistic Realization

realize your whole self and you
will be free
of the circumstances
of this existence and of all
existences in
your multidimensional
form you are divine

4/6/15

919. Let's Pretend

the whole self plays a game
of hide
and seek
with the incarnated personality
this entire
experience
is a game of let's pretend

4/6/15

920. The Prince and the Pauper

you are the prince
and the pauper
and the narrator
and the author

4/6/15

921. You Are a Fiction

you are not the same person
in any way
that you were
ten minutes ago you are created anew
in every second
continuity
is a fiction you maintain

4/6/15

922. Make Your Bid

the energy available to you
now is virtually
unlimited
do not squander it
on safe bets
use it to free
yourself of limitations
use it to open yourself
to your true divinity

4/6/15

923. Your Comfortable Fictions

what would you give
to know
magick is real
would you give up
your comfortable fictions

4/6/15

924. Your Values

the value you give
to others depends
on the value
you give to yourself

4/6/15

925. Your Innermost Being

your innermost being is pure
and immaculate
only by acting
purely and immaculately
can you hope
to approach
your innermost being

4/6/15

926. Falling from Grace

as the day goes on if you fall
out of grace
it is not due
to circumstances
but to the virtue
of your state
of being

4/6/1

927. To Stay in Grace

to hold yourself
in grace
focus on
the divinity within

4/6/15

928. Careful How You Step

he who sees impurities everywhere
feels himself impure
he who grants
himself absolution opening his heart
to love
and compassion
sees the divine in all things

4/6/15

929. No Pride

when you feel pride humble
yourself
there is no pride
in divinity
only love and compassion

4/6/15

930. Welcome All

welcome all
into your temple
with love
and respect

4/6/15

931. Worship All

you must worship divinity
within yourself
and within all
and everything you meet
all of living
is a sacred
act of worship

4/6/15

932. To Honor My Beloved

my beloved resides in my heart
when I denigrate
anyone I denigrate
myself when I
denigrate myself
I denigrate my beloved
to honor my beloved I honor all

4/6/15

933. Namaste

All That Is is mirrored
within the Self
therefore the Self
is mirrored within All That Is

4/6/15

934. Tear Down the Walls

the only way to tear down
these prison walls
is to honor the divinity
within all I meet

4/6/15

935. Released from Prison

to fit in have I made
this place a prison
that is not how
one holds to one's center

4/6/15

936. The Veil is so Thin

the veil
is so thin
the slightest wind
could shift it

4/7/15

937. In Sleep

in sleep
I plumb
the depths
of my existence

4/7/15

938. My Father Called

my father called to me
but when I looked
he was not there
it was only an errant breeze

4/7/15

939. He Called to Me

he called to me
but when I turned
to answer the veil
had shifted back

4/7/15

940. I Built This Prison

I built this prison
that I might find
my freedom
I built it of a seminary
that the truth
behind it would call
to the truth within me

4/7/15

941. Fly Away

I will leave
this prison
on the wings
of my ascension

4/7/15

942. Ladybug

ladybug ladybug
fly away home
bear my love
this message
tell her
I am
with her now

4/7/15

943. The Gifts of Spring

let this spring bring
the flowering
of my heart
let this year bring
the fruition
of my dreams

4/7/15

944. The Energy of Spring

spring bears
the energy of birth
and awakening
if only
we will
release ourselves
from sleep

4/7/15

945. A Journey Back to Source

my life is a journey
back to source
so far I have
traveled without
ever taking a step

4/7/15

946. Swimming the Pond

all of my life I have
been swimming
yet never left
the spring-pool of my source

4/7/15

947. So Far Have I Wandered

so far have I wandered
from my beginnings
yet the distance
I have traversed is measured
in the space
between my mind
and my heart

4/7/15

948. Tired of Mind

when the mind grows
tired then maybe
you will open
the heart

4/7/15

949. Dark of Mind

when the mind is dark
the heart can
provide a light
for it to follow

4/7/15

950. My Love Resplendent

before me stands
my love radiant
in the splendor
of my heart

4/7/15

951. Light of True Worth

may I prove worthy
of the light
my love
does shine on me

4/7/15

952. Inhabit the Heart

within the temple of the heart
there are no distortions
no judgment no limiting
beliefs within the feeling-tones
of the heart there is
only the recognition
of truth in the light of divinity

4/7/15

953. Many Truths

there are many versions
of the truth
some truer than
others
yet every version
is
the truth

4/7/15

954. Only the Heart Knows

truth is a matter
of perspective
the eyes see
wonderful fictions
the mind weaves
artful stories
only the heart knows the truth

4/7/15

955. Lost in the Labyrinth

we are all of us
playing this game
of hide and seek
losing ourselves in the maze
at the heart
of which waits
our own divine Self

4/7/15

956. The Games of Childhood

what cherished children
we are to
the divinity within
playing such
delightful games
peek-a-boo
I see you

4/7/15

957. Riding the Currents

having finally discovered
our Selves we will
ride the currents
of ecstasy and inspiration

4/7/15

958. In Flight

hand in hand
my love
and I
will fly

4/7/15

959. Between Mind and Heart

between mind and heart
exists a gulf
only you
can bridge
when the mind
is guided
by the heart
then you can cross the bridge

4/7/15

960. You Are the Bridge

you are the bridge
the pilgrim crossing
the troll beneath
and the treasure on the far side

4/7/15

961. All Gods

all gods are crutches
true for you only
until you are ready
to dispense with them

4/7/15

962. Fairy Tales

all truths are but
a fairy tale
the purest truth
shall never be spoken

4/7/15

963. The Purest Truth

the purest truth is known
within the heart
and expressed
within all of existence

4/7/15

964. To Know the Truth

to know the truth you must
let go of judgment
still the mind
open the heart
the truth is known within

4/7/15

965. Integrated Truth

when the truth is known
all opposites
are integrated
into a divine whole

4/7/15

966. No Part of the Truth

the truth is
never known
in part
the truth
is only
known
in whole

4/7/15

967. The Whole Truth

the truth cannot
be divided
and analyzed
the truth can only
be known within
the experience
of the truth

4/7/15

968. The Unadulterated Truth

the truth is known
to every child
though they are soon
taught to forget it

4/7/15

969. Release Judgment to Fly

release judgment to be launched
beyond this ever
accelerating
maelstrom spread
the wings of your
divine Self
and take flight

4/7/15

970. The Library of the Quantum Field

in the library of the quantum
field everything
is recorded
the pathway to this library
lies through the temple
of your heart
the doorway is your intuition

4/7/15

971. Within the Library

within the library of akasha
you have access
to all scrolls
that match your vibrational state
simply take
your request
to a librarian

4/7/15

972. Reading Light

the scrolls within the library
of akasha
are read by
the light of the heart

4/7/15

973. Bookcase Ladders

opening yourself to the divine
within allows you
to reach the higher
shelves within the library

4/7/15

974. Reference Librarian

opening yourself further
to divinity
calls out a
researcher who can
access
references
far beyond your reach

4/7/15

975. Library Card

ride the elevator up
and down the floors
of the library
there is nothing you
cannot access
each according
to vibration

4/7/15

976. Your Every Act

as all that exists is one
within the divine
heart of you
your every act transforms
all that exists
bringing it to
a higher level of fruition

4/7/15

977. As Below, So Above

your awakening
to your divine
self brings
a new awareness
to the universe

4/7/15

978. Universal Dawn

the universe is
illuminated
by whatever
light you see it

4/7/15

979. Holographic Change

a change to
the whole affects
every part
a change to any part
affects the whole
and changes
every part

4/7/15

980. Universal Awakening

your awakening
awakens the whole
and each and
every part

4/7/15

981. Universal Opening

open your eyes
to the sight
of infinite
eyes eyes opening opening
opening within eyes
within eyes opening

4/7/15

982. Welcome Home

every such awakening
is a loving
recognition and
a welcoming home

4/7/15

983. Universal Transformation

releasing judgment and ascending
in love you shine
a light reflected
in the heart of all that exists
each light lit
increases the
magnitude of the transformation

4/7/15

984. Self-Illumination

the light
shining within you
the light illumined
ignites reaches out
and within you

4/7/15

985. One Round Further

illumination
is gained
within every
point of time
and existence
in this transformation
All That Is
is a diamond
of infinite
facets

4/7/15

986. Divine Twinkle

in this divine
diamond
of existence
every facet
is a twinkle
in an eye

4/7/15

987. In My Love's Eyes

every
twinkling
reveals
divinity
in my love's
eyes

4/7/15

988. My Love's Eyes Shine

my love's
eyes shine
in every twinkle
of the divine

4/7/15

989. My Love is Found

my love
is found
in every facet
of divinity

4/7/15

990. My Love is a Diamond

my love
is a diamond
of divine
revelation

4/7/15

991. Those Most Angry

those most angry
are most afraid
those most afraid
are most deluded
those most deluded
run from their own
divinity

/7/15

992. Afraid of Your Self

in delusion
many seek
to douse
their own light

4/7/15

993. With Every Shift

with every shift
of frequency
and vibration
you dance from
one probability
to the next

4/7/15

994. Dancing with Your Eyes Closed

the shifting
of probabilities
is the dance
of the ego
it is a ballet
of subtlety
performed
with eyes closed

4/7/15

995. The Dimension of the Solo Dancer

here we perform
a ballet for solo
dancer to music
played on one horn
unknown to us
our dancing partner
is all that
does exist

4/7/15

996. Tango of Judgment and Compassion

in releasing judgment
you gain compassion
for yourself and
others
this is the dance
you came here
to perform

4/7/15

997. Your Lowest Points

your lowest points provide
beauty in their contrast
with your greatest highs
there is divine inspiration
in your ability
to overcome adversity

4/7/15

998. Sinners and Saints

the greatest sinners
make
the greatest saints

4/7/15

999. The Taste of Freedom

only those
imprisoned
can truly appreciate
freedom

4/7/15

1000. The Path of Compassion

when you can appreciate
your lowest moments
you will have transformed
your worst
defeats
into your greatest
successes
in doing so
blazing a trail
to divinity
for all

4/7/15

1001. Our Purpose

our purpose
is to awaken
divinity in even
the most fear-ridden
and delusional
our purpose is
to bring this light
to all the world

4/7/15

1002. Divine Birth

to birth
the higher Self
into the most
abject and
and miserable
of states
is to birth
a universe
of love and
understanding

4/7/15

1003. 3D Illusion

three dimensions
give the illusion
of separation
it is time to step
beyond this illusion
into the freedom
of a higher existence

4/7/15

1004. The Collapse of Time

time is compressing
in relationship
to the rising
frequency
of existence
time is relative
when you cross
the barrier
of three dimensional
existence
time appears
to collapse

4/7/15

1005. Time to Rise

you are the higher Self
experiencing itself
from a perspective
of duality
and separation
when you remember
this it is time
to awaken

4/7/15

1006. You Are Your Creation

you are that
you seek
to become

4/7/15

1007. Don't Hold Yourself Back

to get where you wish
to go stop holding
judgment about
where you are

4/7/15

1008. Acceptance

you must accept
where you are
at in order
to change it

4/7/15

1009. Driven from Now

fear drives you
into the past
or the future
abdicating
your power
in the present
moment

4/7/15

1010. Now Now

what is it
now
that frightens you
now
is where you chose to be

4/7/15

1011. Golden Opportunity

every tribulation
is another opportunity
to shine a light
into the darkness

4/7/15

1012. Coming into Your Own

in your expanding
awareness
of divinity
you are coming
into your own

4/7/15

1013. Homecoming

here is the homecoming
for which you have
reached so long
and longingly
you have been at home
all along all it took
was for you to accept it

4/7/15

1014. The Beauty of This Moment

once you have found
the beauty in
this moment
you would have
it no other way

4/7/15

1015. Welcome Home Love

in the beauty of
this moment
you have found
all you thought lost
welcome
home
my love

4/7/15

1016. Beyond All Expectations

the beauty of this moment
exceeds
all earthly
expectations

4/7/15

1017. Bring It on Home

now to bring it home
work this magick
in all moments
and all circumstances

4/7/15

so'ham
I am that
namaste
ॐ

Ellen Adele Harper is a poet, novelist, performance artist, musician, scientist, activist, and transgender shaman.
http://ellenadeleharper.com/

She can be found on facebook at
https://www.facebook.com/profile.php?id=100079872823238
Instagram
http://www.instagram.com/ellenadeleharper
Twitter
https://twitter.com/EllenAdeleHarp1
Youtube
https://www.youtube.com/channel/UCkkHLjKctUQ64_IRileJdbQ
Tiktok
http://tiktok.com/@ellenadeleharper

www.ingramcontent.com/pod-product-compliance
Lightning Source LLC
LaVergne TN
LVHW080551160826
845677LV00010B/1802

9798363059841